THE EUROPEAN ARMS TRADE

THE EUROPEAN ARMS TRADE

Edited by

Martin Navias and Susan Willett

Nova Science Publishers, Inc.

New York

Art Director: Maria Ester Hawrys
Assistant Director: Elenor Kallberg
Graphics: Denise Dieterich and Kerri Pfister
Manuscript Coordinator: Roseann Pena
Book Production: Tammy Sauter, Benjamin Fung
Circulation: Irene Kwartiroff and Annette Hellinger

Library of Congress Cataloging-in-Publication Data

Navias, Martin and Susan Willett
    The European arms trade / [edited by] Martin Navias and
Susan Willett
        p.   cm.
    Includes bibliographical references and index.
    ISBN 1-56072-300-9 (library bining : alk. paper)
    1. Weapons industry—Europe. 2. Arms transfers—Europe.
    3. Economic conversion—Europe.
    I. Navias, Martin S. II. Willett, Susan.
HD9743.E922E95   1996
338.4'76233'094—dc20   95-48998
                                                                    CIP

Copyright © 1996
Nova Science Publishers, Inc.
6080 Jericho Turnpike, Suite 207
Commack, New York 11725
Tele. 516-499-3103   Fax 516-499-3146
E Mail: Novascil@aol.com

Printed in the United States of America

CONTENTS

Contributors vii

Acknowledgement ix

Introduction *Martin Navias and Susan Willett* 1

Chapter 1:   **A Permissive Practitioner: The U.K.'s Arms Trade Policy**
              Susan Willett 11

Chapter 2:   **German Arms Export Policy**
              Herbert Wulf 31

Chapter 3:   **French Arms Trade and the EC**
              Yves Boyer 47

Chapter 4:   **Devolution of the Nonproliferation Regime?**
              Zachary Davis 57

Chapter 5:   **Financing the Arms Trade**
              Ian Anthony 71

Chapter 6:   **The European Union and the U.N. Register of Conventional Arms**
              Malcom Chalmers and Owen Greene 87

Chapter 7:   **Motives and the Meaning of Guidelines in Arms Export Policy: The U.K. and the Iran-Iraq War**
              Divina Miller 103

Chapter 8:   **Europe, Arms Transfers and the War in Yugoslavia: More Than Technicalities?**
              James Gow 131

Chapter 9:   **Ethics and the European Arms Trade**
              Barrie Paskins 143

Subject Index 157

CONTRIBUTERS

Ian Anthony is a researcher at SIPRI, Stockholm.

Yves Boyer is Deputy Director, CREST Ecole Polytechnique, Paris.

Malcom Chalmers is a lecturer in the Department of Peace Studies, University of Bradford, Bradford.

Owen Greene is a lecturer in the Department of Peace Studies, University of Bradford, Bradford.

James Gow is a lecturer in the Department of War Studies, Kings College, London.

Zachary Davis is a researcher at the Congressional Research Service, Washington D.C.

Davina Miller is a lecturer at the University of Salford, Salford.

Martin Navias is a lecturer in the Department of War Studies, Kings College, London.

Barrie Paskins is a senior lecturer in the Department of War Studies, Kings College, London.

Susan Willett is a researcher at the Centre for Defence Studies, Kings College, London.

Herbert Wulf is Director of Bonn International Centre for Conversion, Bonn.

ACKNOWLEDGEMENT

The chapters appearing in this volume are derived from papers presented at a Workshop on the European Arms Trade held in the Department of War Studies during the winter of 1994. Funding for the workshop was provided by the Social Science Research Council in New York. Additional funding also came from the Department of War Studies Kings College London and the Center for Defence Studies Kings College London. The editors would like to thank Carol Birch for her assistance.

THE EUROPEAN ARMS TRADE: AN OVERVIEW

Martin Navias and Susan Willett

In the bi-polar world of the Cold War arms manufacturers were nurtured by rising demand from both domestic and international markets. Although the global market was dominated by the superpower suppliers, demand was such that European firms secured significant markets particularly in the Third World were cold war ideologies fuelled regional conflicts. However, the collapse of the Cold War system has brought with it fundamental changes in the patterns of supply and demand un the international arms market. As a consequence the arms industry can no longer depend upon the cycles of ever-increasing military expenditures which created the conditions for buoyant demand in the past.

Declining demand has coincided with a climate of concern over conventional weapons proliferation which has generated a more benign attitude towards conventional arms control. The Gulf war provided a grim warning that arms transfers can be dangerous to the long term interests of the supplier nations. The war which cost the allies over $100bn has led to a number of initiatives aimed at limiting conventional arms sales and strengthening controls on proliferation. For all the efforts to limit the conventional arms proliferation there are powerful countervailing forces that are working to undermine such efforts, not least the economic need to find alternative defence markets.

The reversal in the long-term trend from a dynamic arms race to gradual arms control has profound consequences for the European arms industry. This book goes some way towards examining the way in which the major European supplier states are adjusting to the new market conditions and attempts to introduce arms control measures.

BACKGROUND

Foreign sales of European produced defence equipment account for about a third of Europe's total defence production.[1] This is clearly a very large percentage and reflects the importance of arms sales for the European defence industrial base. Globally the trade is far from insignificant. Approximately twenty percent of the total world supply of conventional weaponry derives from Europe. Three states dominate this supply. France, the United Kingdom and Germany provide 85% of the European total. Italy, the Netherlands, Sweden and Spain also vigorously market weaponry though relative to the big three their arms supply quantities are small. The European Union's (EU) major weapons exporters collectively account for $7.3bn (31%) of military transfer agreements to Third World countries in 1992. (Footnote)

The spiralling costs of modern weapons systems and the relatively low levels of domestic demand - compared to that in the United States - has forced European states to place much effort on capturing foreign sales. Traditionally the major markets for European arms apart from the United States have been in the developing world, especially the Middle East and Pacific Asia. European governments have been more than willing to lend political support to arms sales abroad. Government agencies such as the Defence Export Sales Organisation in the UK and the Delegation Generale pour l'Armement have aggressively promoted arms sales in Third World markets sometimes with controversial results. Revelations about French and British military technology transfers to the Middle East during and after the Iran-Iraq war give testimony to that reality.

European arms exports have traditionally been motivated by the specific need to reduce unit costs and maintain production runs. Jobs and foreign currency earnings have also been important incentives for European arms sales. Underlying the economic impetus for arms transfers are also political rationales. West European countries have for decades sought to maximise their autarky in defence production and thus limit their technological, economic and political dependence on the United States.

The balance of trade in armaments which favours the United States has been a constant source of irritation to the major European arms producers, and has defied numerous efforts to reduce what was,

---

[1] Quantitative measures of the global arms market are problematic as there is no universally accepted methodology of accurately recording transfers. For a discussion of these problems see Happe N and Wakeman-Linn (1994) "Military Expenditure and Arms Trade: Alternative Data Sources", in *Peace Economics, Peace Science, and Public Policy* Vol 1, No 4 Summer. Accepting the limitation of available data SIPRI figures will be used to indicate general trends which provide a useful barometer of market performance.

for a long time, a 10 to 1 US trade advantage.[2] In an attempt to improve this deficit, a number of European governments have adopted restrictive practices aimed at discouraging import penetration, while simultaneously stimulating exports. As much of this sensitive trade has fallen outside the remit of the General Agreement on Tariffs and Trade and other mechanisms affecting international commerce, there have been few external restraints on such policies. But despite these measures, the US continues to dominate transatlantic arms transfers and has been accused of undermining European cooperation through its system of bilateral memoranda of understanding with each ally.

No European country can compete in a free arms market with the competitive advantages that the US domestic market bestows on US defence companies. On an economic level the fact that European governments have been willing to maintain their defence industrial bases has proved expensive and inefficient, but has been justified on the grounds of national security interests. However, budgetary constraints and spiralling defence equipment costs has forced a reappraisal of these protectionist policies. By force of circumstances European governments have come to accept the argument that if European companies were prepared to combine their financial, scientific and production resources, there is no technical reason why Western Europe could not compete with the United States.[3] From the mid-1980s tentative moves have been made to harmonise procurement and trade decisions in order to challenge US market dominance.

Collaboration is one way in which European governments have sought to integrate the European industry and to achieve greater economies of scale. The evidence suggests that such programmes come at a premium. Difficulties are encountered in managing such programmes and the economic efficiencies they set out to achieve have rarely been met. [4] The £32bn European Fighter Aircraft project being constructed by Britain, Italy, Germany and Spain is a case in point. Wrangles over specifications led to delays in the commencement of the development phase, German problems over funding the production stage, plus technical difficulties have led to cost overruns and time delays. to tensions between the participants and fears about the projects future.

Building weapon systems in more than one country may make it easier to raise capital but rarely do they lead to savings. Overheads and production facilities are duplicated because few countries are pre-

---

[2] US data on the subject indicates that transfers within Europe amounted to some £208m to £555m in contrast to £1.45bn to £2.2bn in shipments from the US to European allies in 1987 and 1988.

[3] Antony I.(1993) "The USA: Arms Exports" in ed Wulf H. Arms Industry Ltd, SIPRI, Oxford University Press p70.

[4] HCP 247, HMSO, 1991

pared to relinquish production. This is because collaborative programmes are entered into as a means of preserving national industrial capabilities, rather than to rationalise overcapacity and encourage market specialisation which would lead to a leaner and more competitive European defence industry.

Support for cross border integration and a move away from protectionist policies was provided by the IEPG "Action Plan" which was announced in 1986.[5] The IEPG attempted to establish a competitive European defence market through the policy of *juste retour*. but the policy was undermined by the differences in national policies towards the DIB and the disparity in economic and technological performance between the major arms producing companies. Considerable competitive advantage has been bestowed on those defence firms which operate within the context of strong national commitments to defence industrial or technological policies.[6] This accounts for the relative strength of the French and German firms vis a vis the British.

THE EUROPEAN SUPPLIERS IN THE POST-COLD WAR ERA

The end of the Cold War brought with it a dramatic decline in defence expenditures. Within five years global demand for weapon systems had declined by more than 50%. Procurement budgets in both the industrialised and less-developed world are being cut by 3-4% per annum and this trend looks set to continue at least over the medium term given the urgent social and economic pressures that have been generated by the global recession.

The changing conditions of the global arms market are making it more difficult to export the same volume of weapons. The value of exports of major conventional weapons was $21.9bn in 1993, compared to a peak of roughly $46bn in 1987. The lack of hard currency, the growth of indigenous arms industries and the decline of a number of conflicts in the Third world have contributed to the reduction in demand for conventional weapon systems from many traditional Third World recipients. Furthermore, as a consequence of arms control and disarmament agreements, particularly the conventional Forces in Europe (CFE) treaty, governments are off-loading their surplus equipment creating a glut of good quality second-hand equipment, which often directly com-

[5] Independent European Procurement Group (1986) *Towards a Stronger Europe* Report by an independent study team established by the Defence Ministries of Nations of the IEPG, Brussels.

[6] Walker W. and Willett S. (1993) Restructuring the European Defence Industrial Base" in Defence Economics, Vol 4, pp141-160.

petes with new weapons in the marketplace. Against these market trends it is clear that expanding arms exports as a strategy to compensate for declining domestic demand is only a viable alternative for a limited number of the most competitive defence companies.

In this context contraction of the European arms industry has been unavoidable. Facing its worst cyclical downturn since the end of World War 11, defence firms have been forced to lay off defence workers and close down unprofitable plants. Between 1988 and 1990 nearly 300,000 jobs were lost in the European defence industry.[7] The requirements for weaponry by the western European arms industry is likely to be reduced by up to thirty percent by the middle of this decade and as many as 350,000 more jobs are likely to be lost by 1995. [8]

Firms have adopted a number of different strategies in an attempt to adjust to the new market conditions. Some companies are attempting to diversify their production activities in order to reduce their dependence on defence markets either through acquisitions and mergers or through organic growth. The larger defence contractors are forming industrial alliances with both European and international partners to increase their defence global market share and market exposure. [9]

While government directed attempts to restructure the European defence market appear to have failed, market driven restructuring which recognises neither borders nor the need for balanced integration has gathered pace. Several additional developments have contributed to structural adjustment on the supply side. Technological changes shifted the balance of output away from the traditional engineering and metal bashing industries towards electronic hardware and software and the transformation in civil markets (including moves towards the Single European Market) have been forcing European firms to internationalise their operations and reduce their reliance on national procurement. [10]

The main producers of engines, military electronics, missiles and helicopters are in the process of forming joint companies. In 1989 the United Kingdom GEC the defence electronics firm together with the German company Siemens acquired Plessey, GEC also acquired the lucrative parts of the bankrupt electronics firm Ferranti: Royal Ordnance

---

[7] Antony I. and Wulf H. (1992) "The Economics of the West European Arms Industry" in (eds) Brzoska M. and Lock P. *Restructuring of Arms Production in Western Europe* SIPRI, Oxford University Press.p 35.

[8] ibid. p35

[9] There are some excellent detailed accounts of the restructuring of the European defence industry see Brozoska M. and Lock P. (1992) *Restructuring of Arms Production in Western Europe* , SIPRI, Oxford University Press, Wulf H.(1993) *Arms Industry Limited*, SIPRI, Oxford University Press.

[10] Walker W. (1991)"Defence"in Technology and the Future of Europe Global Competition and the Environment in the 1990s (eds) Freeman et al, Pinter Publishers.

purchased by British Aerospace in 1988 is forming a collaborative alliance with GIAT of France to jointly produce ammunition; the German Deutsche Aerospace acquired Dornier and MBB to form the huge aerospace conglomerate DASA ; the French company Aerospatiale has been negotiating with DASA to merge their missile operations, (British Aerospace and Matra of France have been working on a similar deal); in 1990 Aerospatiale and the German firm MBB now part of DASA, merged their helicopter divisions to form Eurocopter SA. In 1989 following several years of negotiation Aerospatiale and Thompson-CSF entered into a joint venture with the Italian firm Selenia to form the missile firm Eurosam.

In a number of these cases merger activity has led to the creation of monopolies at the domestic and European level. By the end of the decade only the most competitive and adaptable companies are likely to survive the process of restructuring, leading to what Walker and Gummett have observed to be an effective cartelization of the European arms market.[11]

Necessary as mergers and rationalisation are to the formation of a globally competitive defence industry the pace of European defence industrial restructuring has been slow in comparison with the process in the USA. US defence industrial sectors have been rationalising over a three to five year period in contrast to European restructuring which is moving over a 10 to 15 year time frame. This is a gap that the European cannot afford if they are to be able to meet the challenge from US competition and survive into the next century.

The absence of a coherent European foreign and security policy is a major factor contributing to the difficulties that European defence companies face in making strategic decisions about their future. The Maastricht Treaty on European Union signed in February 1992 and ratified in 1993 was the first tentative step towards creating a common European foreign and security policy but progress has been slow due to the disparity of opinion on foreign and defence policies by member states. European governments are only just facing up to the reality of the partial or possible total withdrawal of the US military presence from the continent. Key questions about the size and function of NATO remain unresolved and so far the responses to the need for a coherent European foreign and security policy have been faltering.

Despite this apparent lack of direction, the Maastrict Treaty has created new links between the European Union and the revived security institution the Western European Union (WEU) which has considerable implications for the European defence market. As an integral part of the EU, the WEU has the brief to "elaborate and implement decisions

---

[11] Walker W. and Gummett P. (1989) " Britain and the European Armaments market" International Affairs, 55 (3) 419-442.

and actions of the Union which have defence implications". The WEU also provides a bridge between the EU and NATO in its role as the European pillar of the North Atlantic Alliance. In its new capacity the WEU has taken over the role of the IEPG through the creation of a European Armaments Agency with a view to centralizing decision-making within a single European procurement executive. The agency is designed to promote intra-European rather than trans-Atlantic arms trade. These are early days to judge the impact of the WEU on the European arms market.

Traditionally the EC was denied involvement in arms trade issues through Article 223 of the 1958 Treaty of Rome which excludes defence industrial and trade issues from EU jurisdiction, permitting governments to protect national defence industries on national security grounds. But the Single European Act enforced in 1987 is such a strong regulatory structure that it is hard to imagine the defence sector remaining under national control, operating according to completely different sets of rules.[12] Many defence contractors have large operations in civil markets through which EU legislation already exerts considerable influence. For instance the European Commission plays a formal role in approving or prohibiting major corporate mergers, in research and development the Commission runs the Community Framework scheme, which includes a number of defence orientated programmes such as the European research Co-operation Action (Eureka). Within the Commissions remit to aid regions which are suffering acute economic adjustment problems, the Commission has funded defence industrial adjustment projects through the PERIFRA and KONVER programmes. Moreover, the shrinkage in the defence market is reducing the bargaining power of the military specialists, while increasing the proportion of high technology activity that falls under the rules laid down by the Single European Act. As the strength of military institutions weakens, the EC's resolution to remove much of the protection allowed by Article 223 of the Treaty of Rome is likely to increase despite the vociferous opposition to such moves from the UK government.[13]

Efforts are also being made to develop stricter export controls. This can be most clearly seen in the wake of the 1991 Gulf War. Unilaterally Germany, Holland and Belgium all tightened their export legislation. In the United Kingdom the Scott Enquiry into the arms for Iraq scandal and the Foreign Affairs Committee Enquiry into the Pergau Dam affair have stimulated efforts to improve arms control procedures in the UK. The revelations that many European companies supplied

---

[12] Walker and Gummett 1989 op. cit.
[13] Jane's Defence Weekly 4/1/92

equipment to Iraq has led to a tightening of European dual-use technology transfer policies.[14]

The Inter-Governmental Conference in December 1991 proposed an EC wide end-user regime and the establishment of an agency to coordinate, maintain and support national efforts of customs control. However, attempts to suppress Article 223 in order to pave the way towards a common arms control policy was hotly contested by the British government. Undaunted, the EU Commission insists on its prerogatives on dual-use products.[15]

Dual-use transfers are quite significant within the internal market - accounting for around 5% of intra-EC trade.[16] The Commission proposed that dual-use technology transfers within the internal market should not be submitted to controls but that member states should establish a common EC policy of dual-use export controls with third party countries. After much wrangling the Council of Ministers finally ratified the Commissions proposals in 1994. Several measures will thus be introduced which include;

1. A common list of dual-use goods and technologies which are subject to control. The Member States are already working on this, but it will need to be legislated for at a European level.
2. A common list of destinations. It still has to be decided whether this list should be "proscribed" countries or of "special facilities".
3. Common criteria for issuing licenses for exports from the EC.
4. A forum through which to coordinate licensing and enforcement policies and procedures.
5. Explicit procedures for administrative cooperation between Customs and licensing offices throughout the community.

CONCLUSIONS

Three concluding remarks can be made with respect to recent changes in the European arms trade: the first is that, despite moves towards establishing a common arms control regime, the major European arms exporters remain committed to pursuing policies the arms export

---

[14] See Antony et al 1991

[15] A list of products to which the derogation clause of Article 223 applies was drawn up by the Council of Ministers in 1958. This list was based on the 1958 COCOM Munitions List. It has never been amended which implies that a whole range of modern military equipment do not legally fall under Article 223.

[16] Financial Times 17 Feb 1992.

maximisation. A high proportion of European defence output will continue to be exported, and there is great resistance to the curtailment of exports at a time when domestic spending on arms is falling. The present depth of recession in Europe is likely to make governments even more reluctant to curtail arms exports and further exacerbate unemployment. In addition, the desire to raise foreign exchange, to reduce unit costs of equipment required for national defence and to retain high technology sectors of the economy which have relied on defence sales provide a strong incentive to maintain or even increase arms exports.[17] Given these alleged economic advantages, governments may display more discretion in sanctioning exports, but will be reluctant to forsake them.

The second point is that, significant differences in policy and practice have emerged between European governments since the Gulf War. Belgian and the Netherlands have reacted by imposing tighter national export control legislation. In contrast, Britain and France, have maintained their liberal policies of export maximization. In the long-term co-ordinated action by the EU or WEU would reduce the number of centres of decision-making, thereby making international agreements easier to negotiate. It would allow the EU or WEU to exert political and economic leverage over the other suppliers, particularly those who receive economic assistance or who have applied to join the EU.

Despite encouraging moves towards arms control, the form that a common export control policy takes and the pace and effectiveness with which it is activated are still open to dispute. The resistance to export controls should not be underestimated, not least because the export market offers European states the opportunity to support defence dependent industries which is increasingly denied them in civil based sectors under the rules of the internal European market. The existing disparity between European countries' arms export regulations could even become a significant impediment to industrial integration. Countries resisting more restrictive export policies will be loathe to cooperate with their advocates, and vice-versa. On the other hand, it may provide a rationale for greater defence industrial cooperation at the firm level as companies attempt to circumvent tight national export regulations by seeking partners in countries with less restrictive arms export policies.

The third point is that the zeal for tightening controls on the transfer of dual-use technology stands in marked contrast to the aversion to controlling weapons exports. In part this reflects the realization of the threat posed by countries gaining access to the means of producing weapons of mass destruction, and in Europe the inadequacy of past measures which allowed Iraq and some other countries to go so far in

---

[17]See Willett 1991

acquiring nuclear and chemical weapon capabilities. But at the same time, a very real tension exists between the desire to regulate the trade in military-related technologies and the counter pressure to liberalise international trade in civil goods. Member governments of GATT have been stressing the need to stimulate trade in goods and services by removing barriers to the free movement of goods, but for many types of goods there is no clear cut demarcation between military and non-military technologies. Many civil technologies have military applications, including some that are crucial for economic development and growth such as machine tools and production technologies, computers, semiconductors, communication systems, radar and navigational systems. In practice restricting transfers of dual-use technologies and the goal of liberalising trade in general are often contradictory.

To a degree European countries are trying to have their cake and eat it. Abstaining from technology transfer may cause little loss of income while restraining the emergence of new arms competitors. In addition, it avoids tension with the US government, and thus makes it more likely that the flows of US military technology will remain open to Europe. But at the same time, the renewed emphasis on restricting technology flows seems to run counter to the more general trend of the increasing dependence of military on civil technology, so that constraining the diffusion of weapon capabilities is tantamount to constraining the development of civil industries and markets.

Export restrictions which result in a sharp decline in arms transfers depend on a reduced government and economic stake in military production and therefore on a redefinition of national security which downplays self-sufficiency in weapons production. To an extent this is taking place through the restructuring and internationalisation of defence production and by the harmonisation of security and trade policies at a European level. Ultimately the national influence of, and support for, the "military industrial complex" will diminish or be redirected to ease the way for restrictions on weapons exports but this may ultimately depend on the repeal of Article 223 of the Treaty of Rome.

CHAPTER I

A PERMISSIVE PRACTITIONER: THE U.K.'S ARMS TRADE POLICY

Susan Willett
Centre for Defence Studies

The seed ye sow, another reaps:
The wealth ye find, another keeps:
The robes ye weave, another wears:
The arms ye forge, another bears

INTRODUCTION

Until the advent of the Matrix Churchill trial the trade in conventional weapons systems and military related technologies was an uncontroversial issue in the UK. A general consensus prevailed, shared by the leading political parties and trade unions, that arms sales were a good thing for the UK economy as they contribute to the balance of trade, industrial output and employment. In addition, arms transfers were seen as a useful foreign policy lever, maintaining and extending the UK's sphere of influence. It was thought that government responsibility in overseeing arms transactions ensured that British arms were only delivered to reliable client states whose security interests were strongly allied to those of the the British state and its allies. That was until the Matrix Churchill trial in 1993, began a spate of revelations about illegal transfers and shady dealings, evoking questions about the conduct of Her Majesty's Government and UK arms transfer policies. A catalogue of scandals has been revealed in the press which include:

- Disclosures about technology transfers to Iraq by UK companies Sheffield Forgemaster and Matrix Churchill, in violation of the governments guidelines concerning the transfer of "lethal equipment" to Iraq.
- Evidence taken during the Scott Inquiry revealing a less than perfect system of export licensing and the wilful relaxing of guidelines by government ministers in order to secure sales.
- Disclosures by the permanent secretary of the Overseas Development Administration, Sir Tim Lankester, that £234 million in overseas aid has been used as a "sweetener" to secure a £1bn defence sales to Malaysia, in contravention of the government's own regulations concerning the allocation of aid.
- Further revelations of the improper promotion of certain British companies -GEC and BAe - in the £1bn Malaysian arms deal, and the provision of subsidised financing.
- Controversy over the use of bribes to secure the Al Yamamah deal with Saudi Arabia, signed in two parts in 1985 and 1988, the largest arms sale in the UK's history.[1] In 1989 following allegations in *The Observer* of bribes connected to these deals, the National Audit Office (NAO), the government's accounting watchdog, set up an inquiry. In May 1992 Sir John Bourn, NAO's chief handed his report to the Public Accounts Committee. The chair of the committee, Mr Sheldon MP, decided that the report was too sensitive to make public - or even to display to other members of the committee. At the time the report's suppression shocked many MPs. Sheldon justified this move on the grounds that its revelations might adversely affect future sales with Saudi Arabia. According to one source, the allegations in the report referred to British Aerospace paying hundreds of millions of pounds in bribes to the Saudi Royal family and to British middlemen to secure the deal.[2]
- Revelations, by the investigative reporter John Pilger, that the government continues to export arms to the Indonesian regime, which according to eye witness reports has used UK arms against civilians in its war against East Timor, in direct contravention to DTI export guidelines.
- The Custom's decision to investigate into allegations that British companies supplied arms in breach of sanctions to Iran and the former Yugoslavia. The inquiry will investigate the role of Royal Ordnance in helping the German company Heckler and Koch evade the arms embargo and supply Serbian soldiers with small arms and

---

[1] Much speculation exists about the value of the agreement, estimates of between £12bn to £20bn abound.

[2] Ask me no questions, and I'll tell you no lies. The Economist, February 12th 1994, p25.

ammunition. And the role of ICI, Royal Ordnance and Allivane in an illegal European cartel selling arms to Iran during the 1980s.[3]

• Allegations that UK companies were negotiating to supply arms and mercenaries to Azerbaijan.[4]

It would not be unreasonable to assume from these press revealations that the UK arms trade is rife with abuse, malpractice and corruption which has fostered an irresponsible policy of conventional weapons proliferation.[5] Certainly such allegations require investigation - not least to clarify what is true or false. The Scott Inquiry was set up to investigate the evidence for malpractivce in the Matrix Churchill affair. Davina Miller's paper in this volume provides detailed insights into this case. The more general task of examining the UK's role in weapons proliferation has been assigned to the parliamentary sub-committee on Foreign Affairs. The inquiries have promoted the first public debate about the UK's conventional arms trade policy. Critical questions have been raised about the conduct of government, about the lack of accountability and transparency and about the adequacy of existing arms trade control mechanisms. Without wanting to anticipate the results of the Scott Inquiry or the Foreign Affairs Committee this paper explores these issues by firstly examining the issues of accountability and transparency in the UK arms transfer process. Secondly, the economic rational for arms sales is scrutinised. While the final part of the paper profers some policy proposals aimed at establishing a less porous and more responsible arms trade policy.

LACK OF ACCOUNTABILITY AND TRANSPARENCY: THE RELENTLESS PURSUIT OF ARMS EXPORTS

How has a democracy like the UK, ended up with a succession of serious arms trade scandals? This next section attempts to argue that a combination of lack of public accountability and transparency in the arms sales decisions making process, the drive for new arms markets and the general laissez-faire approach of the government combined to produce an unrestrained arms export system which encouraged abuse and corruption within the system.

---

[3]Customs inquiry into arms trade : British companies alleged to have breached weapons sanctions Tim Kelsey and David Keys, The Independent, 3/2/94

[4]ibid.

[5]Proliferation can be defined as the dispersion of military capability and defence related technology. Concern over conventional weapons proliferation has grown in recent years, particularly, since the advent of the Gulf war, and the realisation of the ease with which Iraq acquired the means to build huge conventional forces.

Under the present system of export licensing the Department of Trade and Industry (DTI) is the main department responsible for issuing licenses. When controversy emerges decisions are deferred to the interdepartmental committee (DTI, MoD and FCO) and, as a last resort, to Cabinet committee. Under the present system parliament plays no role in decisions about arms sales. The accountability of ministers to parliament is the chief check on the abuse of power in the UK. However, in practice governments with large enough majorities - as with the Conservatives throughout the 1980s - are rarely accountable to parliament in any stringent sense. This is particularly so in the case of decisions about arms sales, as there is no statutory requirement for consulting or informing parliament about the prospective or completion of arms sales. If an MP wishes to raise questions about arms transfer policies they have to be included in debates on foreign and defence policies and more often than not end up relegated to the bottom of the agenda where larger policy issues are at stake. With no established Bill of Rights, or Freedom of Information Act and/or strong tradition of judicial reviews of legislation or government actions there is little capability for monitoring government accountability in such a sensitive area as weapons transfers. Revelations about malpractice rely upon individual disclosures. The Pergau dam affair only came to light because a senior civil servant took it upon himself, in an act of conscience, to reveal the misuse of aid. A leader in *The Economist* commented that " The details..... are embarrassing enough, but the real scandal is that there is barely any scrutiny of the export of arms, or the equipment used to make them, by anyone except government ministers who approve, or promote, the trade. Arms are not like any other export product. To whom a country sells them is one of the most significant, and controversial, foreign policy issues facing any government".[6]

The lack of parliamentary accountability and the shroud of secrecy which surrounds arms sales has been justified on the basis of commercial confidentiality and respect for the national security of the recipient nations. However, not all major suppliers impose such restrictions. In the US for example, government accountability is strictly adhered to with major export orders openly discussed and voted on in Congress. *The Economist* contends that in the UK "the idea that arms sales should never be scrutinised by anyone, or that arms-export policies should never be publicly debated is preposterous. At the very least an all-party committee of Privy Counsellors.. should review arms deals and report to parliament when the governments own stated policies are breached...Nothing justifies leaving government ministers to operate in the shadow, answerable only to themselves."[7] The outcome of the lack

---

[6]*Exporting British Arms*,The Economist, February, 12th 1994. p20.
[7]ibid.

of accountability is that government ministers ignored their own guidelines in an attempt to maximised export orders.

The drive for export orders was closely linked to fate of the UK's defence industrial base. Spiralling equipment costs made it increasingly difficult to sustain across the board capabilities, particularly, when defence cuts began to eat into the equipment budget in the mid 1980s. International collaboration was one option through which risks and costs could be spread, but the more profitable and short-term solution was to increase exports. At the highest political level ministers became active in arms export promotion and arms sales support institutions were charged with the mission of maximising arms sales.

To this end the UK government put considerable resources into the Defence Export Services Organisation, a department within the Ministry of Defence, first set up by the Labour Party in the 1960s. In defining its role a National Audit report declared that:

> The prime responsibility for defence export sales lies with industry. However, it is government policy actively to support such exports wherever this is compatible with the UK's wider strategic, political and security interests. defence exports allow the maintenance of a stronger defence industrial base than could be sustained by domestic requirements alone, and should result in lower unit cost of production and better value for money in the procurement of defence equipment and services by the Ministry of Defence and our own Forces."[8]

With a staff of over 200, DESO helps companies to obtain licences by coordinating inter-ministerial discussions of sales, it promotes British defence products by organising yearly exhibitions such as the Army and Navy Exhibition held at Aldershot in 1993, it produces the Defence Equipment Catalogue, engages the support of the armed services and defence attaches overseas to help promote sales and provides advice and market surveys. According to Pierre DESO's "clear disposition is to make sales whenever and wherever possible. The style is aggressive and achievement orientated".[9]

The government also paved the way for arms exports by extending credit cover on major deals. In June 1988 an extra £1bn of public money was made available to the Export Credit Guarantee Department specifically to boost large overseas defence sales.[10] The ECGD insures UK exporters against payment defaults from high risk countries.

In maximising arms sales many of the general guidelines for restricting arms transfers to countries or regions, such as human rights violations, internal repression and wars, were overlooked or selectively

---

[8]National Audit Office (1989) Ministry of Defence; Support for Defence Exports, HMSO, London.
[9]Pierre A. opt. cit. p104
[10]The Independent 29/6/88.

applied. Evidence of this permissiveness can be seen in the lifting of the arms embargo against the brutal Pinochet regime; disregard for the ban on the sale of "lethal weapons" to Iran and Iraq enabling the approval of export licences for a whole range of equipment destined for military or military related purposes; indifference to the appalling human rights record of Indonesia and its illegal occupation of East Timor which has been condemned in a number of UN resolutions.[11] Indonesia is just one of many UK customers regularly listed by Amnesty International as a major human rights violator.[12]

The government also turned a blind eye towards questionable "dual-use" trade. It authorised the sale to South Africa of Plessey's mobile military radio system in 1981 and a Marconi surveillance radar system in 1983 in clear contravention of the UN arms embargo. The excuse given was that this equipment had genuine civil application, yet the Marconi radar system was photographed in operation at a military base in the Eastern Transvaal.[13] These actions and the supply of dual-use equipment to Iraq by Matrix Churchill and Sheffield Forgemasters reveal a general failure to screen recipients, apply and monitor end-user controls or exact compliance.

The general atmosphere of laxity towards arms trade controls in the 1980s enabled suppliers to use private arms dealers, obscure shipping lanes, middlemen and false end-user certificates to disguise real destinations in their attempt to secure sales. Often such deals took place with the tacit approval of government or even its active involvement.[14] End-user requirements became less specific as the government relaxed its procedures in pursuit of sales.

These cases illustrate the fact that export guidelines are only as effective as the government of the day intends them to be. During the 1980s the guidelines were subject to manipulation and abuse by a government intent on the sale of weapons at all cost. Afterall the political will to enforce controls has to exist for controls to be effective. Clearly, in the late 1980s, this was not the case. Iraq, Malaysia and Indonesia represented expanding markets for the Thatcher government committed to "batting for Britain" and maximising arms sales. The confidence with which the government was able consistently to circumvent or ignore its own guidelines and established practices can be seen as a func-

---

[11]The UK has supplied the Indonesian regime with a vast array of military equipment ranging from warships and combat aircraft to armoured vehicles and missile launchers. Recent accounts in the press confirm eyewitness reports of UK Hawk combat aircraft in bombing missions on civilian communities in East Timor. See Pilger J. The Death of a Nation, The Weekend Guardian, 12/2/94.

[12]See *Torture in the Eighties*, Amnesty International Publications 1984.

[13]Campaign Against the Arms Trade (1989) *Death on Delivery*, CAAT, London. p19

[14]For a revealing article on the involvement of Royal Ordnance in covert supply operations while it was still state run see The Guardian 29th December 1993.

tion of the impunity guaranteed by the general lack of accountability and transparency in arms export procedures.

THE HIDDEN COST OF THE ARMS TRADE

Britain's continued involvement in the arms trade is, according to one analyst a function of its enduring role as an arms producer. There is "a general sense that having an arms industry is an attribute of an important middle-level power, that the ability to manufacture advanced technology is another source of strength, and that the arms industry may somehow enhance Britain's flexibility in foreign and military affairs"[15] The general consensus, shared by both major political parties and the trade unions, appears to have condoned this approach supporting the received wisdom, that arms sales are a good thing for Britain, as they reputedly contribute to the balance of trade, foreign exchange earnings and employment generation. These alleged economic benefits have had a dominant influence in shaping UK arms sales policy. The costs of adopting a policy of relatively unrestrained arms exports - including short-term budgetary costs and long term economic consequences - are rarely considered in official debates. It is the intention of this section to promote a more balanced appraisal of the economics of arms transfers by emphasising, where possible, the hidden costs of the arms transfers.

In the last few years a number of the assumptions about the economic benefits of the arms trade have been challenged.[16] According to Smith the real returns from arms exports are far less than official statistics lead one to believe. "The financial complexity of the arms export process not only makes it difficult to calculate the real return, but provides a variety of routes for "invisible" cross-subsidization, disguising transfers which would be unacceptable if they were apparent".[17] While not privy to detailed data on cross-subsidization, this section attempts to go some of the way towards revealing where the economic costs lie.

The size of arms production as a percentage of industrial production in the UK is roughly 10%, exports account for roughly 20% of this total and generate 100,000 jobs representing some 2% of manufacturing employment. Arms exports as a percentage of total exports fluctuate according to demand but ranged between 1.1% to 3% during the last

[15]Pierre, A. (1982) *The Global Politics of Arms Sales*, Princeton University Press, Princeton, New Jersey, p102.

[16]Smith R. (1992) *How will limitations affect the overall economies of exporter nations?*, in International Control of the Arms Trade, Oxford Research Group Current Decisions Report No 8, April 1992.

[17]ibid p12.

decade.[18] While notable the contribution to total exports is not that significant and if the value of government subsidies were removed from the annual totals the true contribution of arms exports to the UK's balance of trade and balance of payments is likely to be marginal.[19]

These factors suggest that exports provide only a minimal contribution to the UK's macro-economic performance. It is rather at the microeconomic level that the economic significance of arms exports reveal themselves. The top UK defence companies represent the nations high technology capabilities and defence exports account for a significant part of these companies turnover. These high technology sectors are also the most critical for maintaining high skilled employment.

Undeniably individual defence firms make significant profits from arms exports but the question is where these profits come from. Smith has suggested that they derive from the tax payer rather than export clients.[20] Arms exports are subsidised by the government in a number of ways; through financing the development of the weapon system: by paying for the promotion and marketing of weapons through the MoD's Defence Export Sales Organisation and the use of naval visits etc; providing export credits and insurance through organisations like Eximbank and the Export Credit Guarantee Department (ECGD), which make cheap loans available to the buyer, and compensation to the seller if the buyer defaults on payment, a not unusual occurrence; by giving the recipient aid to finance part of the purchase; and by making political concessions to the buyer to win a deal.

THE DEVELOPMENT OF WEAPON SYSTEMS

It has been estimated that the research and development costs of major weapon systems account for roughly 30% of their unit costs. Despite the fact that all weapon systems are now produced by private companies, the government is the main source of defence R&D funding. Export sales, particularly of major weapons platforms, rarely generate sufficient economies of scale to spread R&D costs significantly. In these circumstances recipient countries are benefitting from state subsidised R&D efforts rather than the other way around as is often claimed.

---

[18]Arms Control and Disarmament Agency (1989) *World Military Expenditures and Arms Transfers*, US Government Printing Office, Washington DC. and National Audit Office *Ministry of Defence: Support for Defence Exports*, HMSO London.

[19]The fact that the ratio of arms exports to total exports has grown in the last few years must be treated with caution as it in part reflects the general decline in UK export performance, rather than any dramatic increase in arms sales.

[20]opt cit.

Table 1. Dependence on Exports of Major UK Defence Contractors
Mid1980s

Firm	Rank	Products	ArmsProduc-tion	Arms exports as a % of production
Bae	7	Aircraft/missiles	54	55
GEC	14	Electronics	35	45
Rolls Royce	39	Aeroengines	40	42
Thorn-EMI	41	Electronics	20	35
Ferranti	44	Electronics	80	40
VSEL	55	Ships	100	30

Source: K. Krause 1992.

DEFENCE EXPORT SERVICES ORGANISATION

The marketing and sales services provided by DESO represent a direct subsidy for the privately owned defence industry. The National Audit Office revealed that DESO had net operating costs of £8.5 million in 1987. In addition a separate unit was set up to promote sales to Malaysia, what this cost and who this was accountable to has yet to be revealed. These costs are paid for by the British tax payer and yet DESO is not accountable to parliament, and operates under a shroud of secrecy.

CREDIT FINANCING AND LOANS

The defence share of export credits has grown to about half of the total provided by the Export Credit Guarantee Department.[21] In the late 1980s the ECGD was provided with an extra £1 billion to provide support for exports, including significant arms related exports to Iraq.[22] As a result £940 million worth of claims have been paid or are under consideration.

The National Audit Office has drawn attention to certain problems which arise with credit financing arrangements "in assessing alternative options, the full costs and benefits of different financing arrangements are not fully addressed. If this is not done there is a risk that what might appear to be a good deal is, owing to credit finance ar-

---

[21]Leader Comment,*Critical Questions*, The Guardian, 17/2/94

[22]It is thought that significant losses have arisen out of the shady dealings with Iraq. This is an area which could be investigated.

rangements, is not actually the best option".[23] For instance problems may arise as a result of movements in the exchange rate affecting the ability of the purchasing nation to repay "loans". Another danger, illustrated by the case of Iraq, and Iran before that, is that a country which is classified as an ally one moment can rapidly turn into the "next Hitler", thus leaving loans unpaid. The cumulative costs of writing off bad foreign loans for military sales is ultimately borne by the tax-payer.

OFFSETS

The real return on the arms transfers is obscured by "offsets". Although statistics on the total value of offset arrangements entered into by UK firms in a given year is not publicly available, it is clear that this practice substantially reduces the net benefits of arms sales to the UK economy. A number of sources indicate that for most sales outside of the Middle East, most notably in the Asian Pacific, a 100% offset target has become standard practice in arms deals.[24]

Essentially offsets can be direct or indirect. Direct offsets comprise the participation of the recipient nation's industry in some aspect of the contract for supplying foreign defence equipment. For instance, the acquisition of a tank might involve final assembly in the purchasing country together with subsequent repairs and servicing.[25] Indirect offsets involve goods and services distinct from the purchase of the specific foreign defence equipment. Examples include the supplying nations government or contractor agreeing to purchase some other item of defence equipment or civil goods from the recipient nation eg Tornadoes for oil, which then have to be marketed separately. In some cases the resale value of goods may be substantially less than the notional value in the contract. In addition, "offset purchases" from the recipient country may require accepting poor-value products, transferring technology, or investing in established industries in the buying country, which may be charged against the aid budget.

Offsets can be viewed as both a marketing tool and the means of financing weapons sales, but they are not greatly liked by industry. In an increasingly competitive market contractors have been willing to go along with these arrangements to secure sales, but such arrangements

---

[23]NAO (1992) *The Risks to Value for Money in Defence Procurement* Paper presented to the 15th Conference of Commonwealth Auditor Generals, p8.

[24]See for instance Hartung,W.(1994) *Conflicting Values, Diminishing Returns: The Hidden Costs of the Arms Trade*, monogragh, World Policy Institute, New York.p15

[25]Typically offsets which include licensed or joint production of a weapon system or component involves the transfer of technology which contributes to the process of conventional weapons proliferation.

often run counter to their long term business interests. While prime contractors may benefit from immediate sales, sub-contractors often lose their business to coproducers in the recipient nation. In this manner the supplier nation exacts an industrial and employment cost. For instance the US General Accounting Office has calculated that although the Korean Fighter Program will result in more US jobs gained than lost, the balance is very delicate. And in the long run the fear is that the transfer of US aerospace technology is likely to result in the creation of a formidable competitor in the future.

A US survey of major arms sales during the period 1980-87 by the Commerce Department's Bureau of Economic Analysis identified $35bn in military exports involving offset arrangements. The reported value of the offset deals was an estimated $20bn, or more than 57% of the value of the original transfers.[26] So far there has been no similar enquiry in Britain into the scale of offsets commitments or their opportunity costs. But UK firms are increasingly involved in offset arrangements which suggests that far less of the reported economic advantages in arms sales actually accrues to the UK than existing arms sales data leads one to believe.

The National Audit Office has noted that there are several risks involved in offset arrangements for both supplier and recipient nations.[27] When acquiring foreign defence equipment, offsets are a means by which the purchasing government obtains compensating work for their national industries and products. Financially and politically these deals can look very attractive to the recipient nation. However, it is always hard to evaluate whether or not the purchaser's national industry would have received the work anyway. And such agreements are difficult to control and monitor.

In the US there is growing concern that "offsets are economically inefficient and that they foster foreign competition with US manufacturers....Cynics might also add that they appear to be a vehicle for pork-barrel politics and petty corruption on a grand scale".[28] Since offsets frequently involve taking business from UK firms and giving it to foreign suppliers, they ultimately diminish the net economic benefits of arms sales to the UK economy.

---

[26]Hartung op. cit. p15

[27]NAO, op.cit. pp 8-9.

[28]Lora Lumpe (1994) *Sweet Deals and Low Politics: Offsets in the Arms Market*, FAS Public Interest Report Jan/Feb.p1

AID FOR ARMS TRADE

The Pergau dam scandal has finally given substance to the suspicion that overseas aid has been used to "sweeten" arms transfers. The
amount offered for the "uneconomic" Pergau project represents more
than 25% of the total value of the original deal struck by Margaret
Thatcher and the Malaysian Prime inister Dr Mahathir, in 1988.
However since the MoU was signed Malaysia has failed to follow
through on the orders the Tornados (preferring MiG-29s) or frigates, in
value terms these items would have represented a significant part of
the £1bn order. This suggests that the aid provided to secure the deal
now represents a much larger percentage of the total value of the deal,
thus resulting in a much poorer rate of return to the UK economy. It
would appear that the main beneficiaries will be the companies such
as Balfour Beatty, Trafalgar House and GEC-Marconi who are bidding
for construction contracts for the dam, while the British tax payer, already overburdened by tax increases, will be the ultimate loser.[29]

HIDDEN COSTS PROLIFERATION AS THREAT

An increasing proportion of arms transfers take the form of licensed
production, offsets and joint ventures. In a buyers' market the pressure
to enter into such agreements is considerable. Essentially such arrangements represent technology transfer and have long term implications
for proliferation, competition and security. Unrestrained arms transfers
are linked to conventional weapon systems proliferation and the
growth of aggressive regional powers that may pose a potential threat
to the UK in the long-run.

The most notable security implication of co-production deals is the
irrevocable transfer of defence industrial technologies and manufacturing know-how not only in conventional weapons but also for the possible development of long range missiles and weapons of mass destruction. In addition, co-production deals could have the effect of ferment-
ing regional militarism through the proliferation of conventional
weapons, while eroding suppliers' control over transferred military capabilities. They foster a more competitive arms market which will
lead to less discriminate sales and still more technology transfer in the
future. While the expanding numbers of arms suppliers profoundly
complicates efforts to achieve limits on international arms transfers
through negotiated arms control or multilateral arms embargoes.

The most costly effect is when a client turns enemy and poses a direct security threat. This has happened twice to the UK in recent his-

---

[29]Vivek Chaudhury and Simon Beavis *Inquiry urged into aid "sweetners"*, Guardian, 12/2/94

tory in Iran and Iraq. The most costly being the UK involvement in the 1991 Gulf War which has been estimated at £2.5bn.[30] Once contributions were made from allies the bill for the taxpayer was greatly reduced. But the point here is that the total cost to the allies of containing the effect of proliferation was in excess of $80bn. All the major suppliers, including the UK have been implicated in supplying the weapons and technologies, which enabled Saddam Hussein to build up the fourth largest army in the world. In the 1980s the Iraqi arms market was seen by many, including the UK government as a bonanza. But in the end it was the suppliers that had to pay the price of proliferation.

Without detailed data assessment of the economic costs of the arms trade are speculative. However, even on the limited evidence which exists it can be asserted with relative confidence that at best UK arms transfers provide marginal short-term gains for the UK economy. Once all factors are taken into account, including the cost of taxpayer subsidies for arms exports, the impact of industrial offset programmes: the role of arms transfers in fostering regional arms races that can result in additional defence expenditures: the opportunity costs for the UK and the international economy of promoting arms sales instead of commercial activities results in a long-term net cost to the UK economy.

If the economic advantages of arms sales are more illusion than reality why then does the state continue to promote arms exports? There are very clearly substantial vested interests in the defence industrial base which have over time developed a powerful lobbying force able to exert considerable influence over government decisions both on procurement and trade. Emerging evidence suggests that in the Malaysian deal the British government agreed to a secret pact to subsidise exports for British Aerospace and GEC, both companies having curried favoured status with the government.

POLICY RECOMMENDATIONS

There is clearly a need for a major review of UK export policies. Such a review coincides with a number of national and international initiatives designed to improve arms transfer controls in the post Cold War era. In the section below a number of recommendations are listed aimed at improving UK policy.

---

[30]National Audit Office (1992) *Ministry of Defence:The Costs and Receipts Arising from the Gulf Conflict*, HMSO, London, p1

TRANSPARENCY AND ACCOUNTABILITY

Recent disclosures suggest a clear case for greater transparency and accountability in the UK's arms trade policy. At the very least there should be an all-party committee which should regularly review arms deals and report to Parliament when government regulations are transgressed.

While the UK government has to be commended as a prime mover behind the creation of the UN Register on Conventional Weapons it should be encouraged to support moves towards prior notification of arms sales and the register of all production capabilities.

AN ARMS SALES POLICY AUDIT

Using the full investigatory and auditing powers at its disposal the government should conduct a comprehensive arms sales policy audit that reviews the full costs of the UK government's efforts to promote arms sales, and take into account the potential costs to UK security of continuing the policy of unrestrained conventional weapons exports. The findings of this policy should be used as a guide for reforming and improving UK arms transfer policies and practices.

EXPORT CONTROLS

The results of the governments relatively unrestrained approach to arms sales and the laxity with which arms export guidelines have been interpreted, suggests the need for a more restrictive domestic arms export policy and greater efforts in establishing multilateral export controls for conventional weapons. End-user certificates should be issued more often and arms transfers should be effectively monitored. Compliance should be enforced through the threat of substantial fines or sanctions.

At an international level the government should be encouraged to reinaugurate the P5 or the P4 talks (if China will not re-engage) on arms transfer restraint and regional arms control initiatives. New types of weapons should be restricted to regions where they are not already present. Equally the government should be persuaded to support the moves towards greater harmonisation of European arms export controls. Endorsing the moves towards greater restriction and control as advocated by the German's, rather than holding out for the more laissez-faire policies at present advocated by both the British and French governments.

OFFSETS ARRANGEMENTS

The DTI should be required to notify Parliament of coproduction or licensed production of major weapon systems or components with any country, and to explain why it is in the interest of national security to provide the country with an independent arms capability. The report should list the articles to be produced, how many and by whom, restrictions on third-part transfers, an a description of controls incorporated into the agreement to ensure compliance with this. The report should be made available to the public so that coproduction trends can be monitored by independent analysts. In addition an "impact statement" should be required for each coproduction deal, examining the consequences for regional security, trade and employment.

The government should develop a set of guidelines on coproduction to ensure compliance with coproduction agreements. Parliament should be notified of the details of all coproduction MOUs. Notifications or reports should include a section on whether compliance related provisions have been made.

CODE OF CONDUCT ON ARMS EXPORTS

The government should support the proposals for a British and European Code of Conduct on the Arms Exports. The premise of such legislation is that states which are not democratically elected, that abuse human rights, or are at war, are inherently less stable. And states which do not share limited information on weapons procurement with the UN register on Conventional Arms are innately untrustworthy, therefore such states should be denied arms transfers. As a general guideline in international negotiations on multilateral conventional arms control the UK government should be encouraged to organise around the highest common factor such as the German standards, and not the watered down level of minimum controls which the UK government has been emphasising in recent debates with international allies.

CONCLUSION

On the domestic front there is a need for more public notice of arms transfers and destinations, and a stricter criteria about the supply of arms to countries engaged in proliferation or arms build ups. Although Britain is a highly developed democracy the tradition of secrecy and governmental privilege which surround defence matters plus the vested interests of the "Military Industrial Complex", means there is little

public accountability in the decision making process over arms transfers. Revelations about malpractice more often than not rely upon individual disclosures. The Pergau dam affair only came to light when the
Permanent Secretary of Foreign Affairs took it upon himself to reveal
the misuse of aid as a sweetener for defence contracts in direct contravention of the guidelines covering the terms of donation of British aid.
A leader in the Economist commented that

> The details ... are embarrassing enough, but the real scandal is that there is
> barely any scrutiny of the export of arms, or the equipment used to make
> them, by anyone except government ministers who approve, or promote, the
> trade. Arms are not like any other export product. To whom a country sells
> them is one of the most significant, and controversial, foreign policy issues
> facing any government".[31]

If parliament continues to play no formal role in the decision making process, and there is no statutory requirement for it to be either con-
sulted or informed about current or future sales the misuse of power in
arms sales is likely to continue.

On the issue of arms restraint the British government has consistently expressed a preference for multinational approaches to the control of arms transfers in the belief that the British share of the global
arms market is too small for a unilateral control effort to make much
effect. To its credit in the promotion of multinational approaches, the
UK played a prominent role in establishing the UN Arms Trade Register which was formerly instituted in December 1991. But as Spear has
observed British enthusiasm for greater international transparency in
arms sales sits uneasily with Britain's unwillingness at the domestic
level to reveal details of arms transfer agreements.[32] Spear is also cynical about the possibility of a change in UK arms trade policy in the
near future. She anticipates a continuation of Britain's "ambivalent "
approach of appearing concerned about the global increase in conventional arms spending while maintaining a policy of aggressively marketing British wares in the global arms bazaar.[33]

Export restrictions which result in a sharp decline in arms transfers
depend on a reduced government and economic stake in military production and therefore on a redefinition of national security which down
plays self-sufficiency in weapons production. The irony for the British
government is that to an extent this is taking place despite their am-
bivalence towards arms control through the restructuring and internationalisation of defence production and by the harmonisation of secu-

---

[31]*Exporting British Arms,*The Economist, February, 12th 1994. p20.

[32]Joanna Spear(1990) *British and conventional arms transfer restraint* in UK arms control in the
1990s M. Hoffman Manchester University Press. p174.

[33]Spear J. op cit. p 171.

rity and trade policies at a European level. Ultimately the national influence of, and support for, the "military industrial complex" will diminish or be redirected to ease the way for restrictions on weapons exports but this will ultimately depend on the repeal of Article 223 of the Treaty of Rome, which the UK government has so vigilantly upheld.

APPENDIX

THE UK ARMS MARKET

One of the major problems in undertaking a study of the British arms trade is the lack of accurate information As Pierre has found in the past the "whole subject is shrouded in secrecy".[34] Data on the arms trade is notoriously difficult to access and what does exist often provides only a partial picture. For example in the annual figures released in the UK Statement on Defence Estimates, there is no explanation provided regarding the proportion of weapons transfered as opposed to services, or to whom the sales are to be made. Only the regional destinations in aggregate figures are provided. But it is not clear whether the figures include offset or counter-trade agreements which account for an rising number of transactions. In order to obtain more disaggregated data it is necessary to turn to sources such as the Arms Control and Disarmament Agency, the Stockholm International Peace Research Institute, and International Institute of Strategic Studies. Although these sources also have their limitations they nevertheless provide more detailed information than can be derived from largest regional market accounting for 60% of all UK arms transfers. official sources. According to official data in 1992 the UK exported just under £2bn of military equipment The Middle East and North Africa is the UK's largest regional market accounting for 60% of all UK arms transfers.

Third World markets accounted for roughly £8.6bn worth of sales between 1985-92.[35] The Middle East and North Africa accounted for £5.8bn during this same period. Unlike the United States the UK government imposes few restrictions on the types of weapon systems it exports to the Third World, consequently state of the art equipment used the UK's armed forces are regularly promoted at international arms sales, and are readily available to those who can afford them.

---

[34]Pierre A. (1982) *The Global Politics of Arms Sales,* Princeton University Press, Princeton, NJ.
[35]SIPRI, *SIPRI Yearbook 1992,* Oxford University Press, 1992 p 199

Table 1. Distribution of UK Arms Transfers

Destination	1985	1986	1987	1988	1989	1990	1991	1992
NATO & W. Europe	247	209	254	412	470	396	442	350
M.E & N. Africa	284	412	32	685	1569	1207	1156	851
Other Africa	155	68	45	38	34	39	31	85
Asia & Far East	73	100	260	199	306	295	220	199
Latin Amer & Carib	54	38	41	37	28	46	35	21

Source: Statement on the Defence Estimates,HMSO 1991.

Table 2. UK Exports of Defence Equipment

	1985	1986	1987	1988	1989	1990	1991
Total deliveries*	813	826	1233	1369	2408	1980	1862
Armoured vehicles and parts	127	87	56	59	52	70	66
Military aircraft and parts	174	192	326	813	1524	1206	1367
Warships	4	12	61	26	41	3	8
Guns, small arms and parts	155	133	214	133	84	65	48
Guided Weapons, missiles	55	39	143	112	276	143	58
Ammunition	85	209	287	102	200	315	115
Radio and radar apparatus	128	115	94	81	133	123	135
Optical equipment & trainingsimulators	85	40	49	43	97	54	49
Additional aerospace equip**	940	1312	1853	1406	717		
Aircraft, guided weapons and parts	396	566	1056	534	84		
Aircraft equipment	316	451	523	574	367		
Aero-engines and parts	201	270	274	288	259		
Space equipment	27	25	..	10	7		

Source: *Statement on Defence Estimates 1993*

*   *These figures are supplied by the Customs and Excise and only refer to actual deliveries of equipment that have passed through the Customs barrier.*
** *These figures are based on estimates of additional military exports compiled by the Society of British Aerospace Companies. Exports for collaborative projects are excluded.*

The table above provides a breakdown of the major types of equipment exported.

According to SIPRI in 1992 the UK transferred military technology to 32 countries in total, 20 Third World countries and 12 industrialised countries. The table below provides details of the destinations and types of weapon systems that were transferred in 1992.

Table 2 UK Exports of Defence Equipment

	1985	1986	1987	1988	1989	1990	1991
Total deliveries*	813	826	1233	1369	2408	1980	1862
Armoured vehicles and parts	127	87	56	59	52	70	66
Military aircraft and parts	174	192	326	813	1524	1206	1367
Warships	4	12	61	26	41	3	8
Guns, small arms and parts	155	133	214	133	84	65	48
Guided Weapons, missiles	55	39	143	112	276	143	58
Ammunition	85	209	287	102	200	315	115
Radio and radar apparatus	128	115	94	81	133	123.	135
Optical equipment & training simulators	85	40	49	43	97	54	49
Additional aerospace equip**	940	1312	1853	1406	717		
Aircraft, guided weapons and parts	396	566	1056	534	84		
Aircraft equipment	316	451	523	574	367		
Aero-engines and parts	201	270	274	288	259		
Space equipment	27	25	..	10	7		

Source: Statement on Defence Estimates 1993

CHAPTER 2

GERMAN ARMS EXPORT POLICY

Herbert Wulf
Centre for Defence Studies
King's College, London[*]

Despite contrary political declarations and possibly even intentions, Germany's arms industry inevitably but almost inadvertently moved the country into a prominent place among arms exports. According to SIPRI, Germany ranked third in global exports of major conventional weapon systems in 1992 and ranked second among the exporters that reported to the United Nations Register of Conventional Weapons for the same year. The Government's circumvention of existing laws and "liberalisation" of export controls (in the 1970s and, especially, in the first half of the 1980s) is one only part of the story. The deeply rooted cause of export-oriented arms production is the internationalisation of the country's economy. Once a country embarks on the production of weapons, economic considerations (economies of scale as well as companies` business interests) lead unavoidably to an explicit arms transfer policy. German arms exports are the logical consequence of the Governments` decision to produce major weapon systems, to the extent possible, domestically. Thus, the reality of arms exports is often in stark contrast to the declared official policy.

A foreign observer introduced his analysis of German arms export policy by correctly describing this dilemma: "The German phrase *unvermeidliches Uebel* (necessary evil) captures the essential dilemma of the Federal Republic's arms transfer policies; it could also be translated, ´unavoidable evil`. Both are apt descriptions of the German approach to the transfer of arms, especially since the 1960s."[1]

---

[*] Paper prepared for the workshop on the European Arms Trade.
Dr Herbert Wulf is Director of Bonn International Center for Conversion (BICC).

[1] Frederick S. Pearson, Necessary Evil: Perspectives on West German Arms Transfer Policies, Armed Forces & Society, Vol. 12, No. 4, 1986, pp. 525-552.

EXPORT REGULATIONS: RESTRICTIVE RULES

Two laws, both passed in 1961 and subsequently amended several times, regulate the arms exports.[2] The Weapons of War Control Act (Gesetz über die Kontrolle von Kriegswaffen, KWKG) regulates exports of weapons and the Foreign Trade Act (Außenwirtschaftsgesetz, AWG) regulates exports of military-related technology and armaments.[3] Attached to both laws are lists of goods: a "list of weapons of war" and an "export list". Despite the fact that these laws are among the most restrictive in the world, the FRG has for the past two decades been counted among the major arms exporters.

The Constitution of the FRG, written in 1949, explicitly prohibits, as a response to the experience during the war years, actions that would threaten peaceful co-habitation among its peoples, especially actions to prepare for or carry out an offensive war. Article 26, paragraph 2 of the Constitution specifies that "weaons intended to be used for war" can only be produced, transported and traded with the permission of the Federal Government.

The two laws mentioned above are a result of the constitutional restrictions and a response to West German rearmament. According to the Weapons of War Control Act, the Government *must* refuse an export licence if there is reason to believe that it would be detrimental to international relations, if there is a danger that the weapons will be used in a peace-threatening action, particularly an offensive war, or if there is reason to believe that the exports would not be in accordance with the responsibilities of the FRG under international law.

Germany follows a liberal policy in its foreign trade. As a rule, unless explicitly forbidden, foreign trade does not require a government licence. The Foreign Trade Act, which regulates all international trade, stipulates regarding "war-related arms and other arms" (kriegswaffennahe und sonstige Rüstungsgüter) that export licences *can* be refused to guarantee the security of Germany, to prevent disturbance of the peaceful co-habitation of its peoples, or to prevent significant disturbance in Germany's international relations. As is obvious, these provisions in the laws enable differing interpretations.

Both to guide the administrative decision-making process and to find a compromise line in the controversial area of arms exports, the Government initially established so called "political principles" in 1971. These guidelines were very strict, dividing the world into four categories of countries: NATO countries that could import weapons from

---

[2] This sections draws on Herbert Wulf, The Federal Republic of Germany, in: Ian Anthony, SIPRI, (ed), Arms Export Regulations, (Oxford University Press: Oxford, 1991), pp. 72-85.

[3] The relevant laws and latest amendments are reprinted in Elmar Matthias Hucko, Außenwirtschaftsrecht, Kriegswaffenkontrollrecht, (Bundesanzeiger: Köln, 1992).

Germany; countries that fell under COCOM regulations; countries in areas of tension that would not receive any weapons; and "other countries" where no weapons were to be exported, except in individual cases as a result of special political considerations.

In 1982, the currently existing guidelines were introduced. Compared to the 1971 guidelines, the 1982 principles contained several important changes:

- Regarding NATO countries, the problem of co-production programmes was addressed. As a result of the changes, co-production interests have priority over German export restrictions. Thus, components produced in Germany could be exported by co-production partners (the tornado fighter aircraft being one example).
- The "areas of tension" criteria was abandoned and replaced by the formulation that "the supply of weapons of war and war-related armaments goods must not heighten existing tensions".
- As a general principal, exports of weapons of war are not permitted, unless the vital interests of Germany—such as foreign and security interests—call for an exception. Jobs in the arms industry do not qualify as such vital interests.
- An end-user certificate is required.

DUBIOUS EXPORT DEALINGS AND THE CHANGES OF THE LAW

At the beginning of 1989, after heated public debate about exports by West German companies of technology to produce chemical weapons in Libya, the Government proposed to amend the existing laws to enable tighter controls, especially over the exports of weapon-production technology.[4] Several amendments were passed in 1990. Nevertheless, after the Iraq invasion of Kuwait it became publicly known that German companies had supplied military relevant equipment and dual-use technology to Iraq and had assisted in building up Iraq's arms industry. While several cases of these transfers are still pending in courts and others have been recognised as illegal, many of the involved companies in fact exported on the basis of valid Government licences.

---

[4] See the Government report to Parliament on the exports to Libya: Deutscher Bundestag, Plenarprotokoll 11/126, 17 Feb. 1989, pp. 9259-311.

Bearing in mind that the very idea of a German arms industry is controversial,[5] these arms deals focused critical attention on companies in the arms sector at a time when they were preparing to place even more emphasis on exports in order to compensate for declining domestic orders. For many, the names of German arms conglomerates like Flick, Krupp, Messerschmitt, Blohm & Voss, and Daimler Benz—some of which no longer produce arms—still have the ring of Germany's role in the two world wars. Criticism, of course, stems from the legacy of their role in fuelling German militarism.

Yet the exports of technology with military application to Libya and Iraq do not mark the beginning of controversial or dubious arms deals. On the contrary, the post World War II history of West German arms exports could be written as a history of scandals. A few examples suffice to illustrate this point.

- The fighter aircraft Alpha Jet was officially declared a trainer to allow exports to Nigeria.
- Licenses for the export of many fighting ships, such as fast attack craft, frigates, and submarines—although officially called an exception to the rule—were usually granted with the explicit public reasoning that jobs in the yards were at stake.
- Many countries—including Burma, Saudi Arabia, Sudan, and Thailand— obtained licences to produce machine guns.
- The Government-owned shipyard HDW exported blueprints for diesel-driven submarines to South Africa, a UN embargoed country.
- Submarines were exported to Chile at a time when the Pinochet Government was considered an outcast by German Foreign Policy.[6]
- More recently, former East German NVA equipment has been shipped to numerous countries (including Uruguay, Indonesia and Turkey) irrespective of the human rights situation in these countries.

As a consequence of intensive domestic and international criticism after the Libya and Iraq affairs, several amendments of the existing

---

[5] It is interesting as a side note that the arms industry in Germany usually is referred to as „arms industry" rather than as "defence industry", as is the case in the United Kingdom and the United States.

[6] For the political background and other transfers see Michael Brzoska, Rüstungsexportpolitik (Haag & Herchen: Frankfurt, 1986) and Herbert Wulf, Waffenexport aus Deutschland (Rowhlt: Reinbek 1989).

laws and control mechanisms were passed in 1990 and 1992.[7] The most important include the following:

- In addition to the COCOM country list, two other lists (lists H and I) were added as an appendix to the Foreign Trade Act to introduce special controls for sensitive countries. At present, 34 countries are on the H list while 9 countries that did not sign the NPT are on the I list.
- A "catch all clause" has been introduced for dual-use goods. An exporter of a dual-use item has to declare that his product will not be used in the military sector. Otherwise an export licence is required, even if the product is not on the trade list.
- An exporter has to declare who in the company's management bears responsibility for the exports.
- Legal penalties for illegal transfers have been toughened.
- A new Federal exports office has been established and the number of customs and inspection staff increased.

PATTERNS AND HISTORY OF ARMS TRANSFERS

In the absence of a diversified arms industry, until the mid-1960s arms transfers consisted mainly of outdated US weapons, exported or donated by West Germany, to assist the country in the Cold War struggle against the German Democratic Republic.[8] Arms sales were an instrument to enforce the Hallstein Doctrine which tried to foreclose diplomatic recognition of the German Democratic Republic. Many of these deals had been carried out more or less secretly, often clandestinely; legal reservation had been disregarded. Furthermore, firms began to participate in military co-production projects within NATO and as subcontractors for US companies.

German arms exports, like supplies from other major Western exporters increased rapidly in the 1970s. The market shifted somewhat from Western to Third World customers. Third World sales also shifted as a result of sales bans ("area of tension" regulations) in the late 1960s, from predominantly Middle Eastern to Latin American, African, and Asian countries.

Later, as oil wealth accumulated in the OPEC countries, West Germany's Middle Eastern sales revived, totalling about one third of its

---

[7] A detailed analysis of the export regulations, including the latest amendments of the law is Hartmut Bebermeyer (ed), Deutsche Ausfuhrkontrolle 1992, (Bernard & Graefe: Bonn, 1993).

[8] For the early period see Ulrich Albrecht, Der Handel mit Waffen (Hanser: München, 1971) and Helga Haftendorn, Militärhilfe und Rüstungsexporte der BRD (Düsseldorf, 1971).

arms exports from 1973 to 1977, according to ACDA statistics. Although export guidelines and official Government policy continued to underline German preference for sales to NATO countries, sales to the Third World were four times higher than those to NATO during the 1970s. The sales increase was mainly due to a high concentration on a small number of dominant regional powers—Nigeria, Iran, Brazil, and Argentina.[9]

Up to the beginning of the 1980s, some 70 countries outside NATO had imported weapons, spares, and other military equipment or weapons production technology from West Germany.[10]

As in other countries, in the early 1980s arms exporters in Germany experienced stagnating and somewhat diminishing foreign sales. This was not a consequence of a changed policy but exclusively a result of the reduced purchasing power of Third World weapon customers. When the Conservative-Liberal coalition took power in 1982, exports were de facto further liberalised without, however, changing the two relevant laws or the 1982 governmental guidelines. Several arms deals illustrate this trend in policy.

In 1983, a formal agreement for arms co-operation was signed with Saudi Arabia—the first such agreement with a developing country. The Government, while hinting at the need for secure oil supplies, called the agreement an "expression of our vital interest in the stability of the Gulf region."[11] At the same time, in July 1983, the Government amended the weapon list and removed, for example, helicopters and aircraft without sophisticated electronics from the list. Export of such equipment was in effect liberalised.

In 1985 the Government announced that the Association of South-East Asian Nations (ASEAN) countries would be treated as equal to NATO countries. In other words, export of weapons and other military-related equipment and technology were no longer restricted.

During the following years the Government proceeded further in its export promotion. Pressed by the British Government, it agreed to partly finance the sale of co-produced Tornado fighter planes to Jordan. Only after massive public protest was the promise of credit financing withdrawn, to the annoyance of the Thatcher Government. In covert form, the credit guarantee was then given by a bank owned by the state of Bavaria, although the whole export deal fell through as a result of Jordanian financial difficulties.

---

[9] Fred Pearson, op. cit.

[10] Detailed empirical evidence in Herbert Wulf, Waffenexport aus Deutschland, op cit.

[11] Deutscher Bundestag. 10. Wahlperiode, 165. Sitzung, 17 Oct. 1986, pp. 12335-36.

million

US $

	1988	1989	1990	1991	1992
developing countries	300	280	800	500	400
industriealized countries	950	570	850	2010	1580

Figure 1. German Exports of Major Conventional Weapons
In Millions of $US

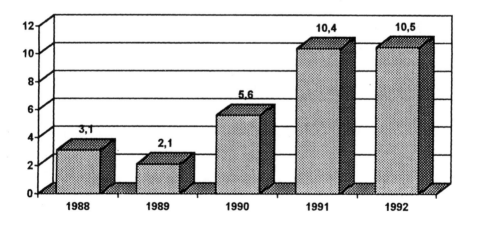

Figure 2. Share of German Exports
In Global Trade of Major Convention Weapons

Source: SIPRI Yearbook 1993, p. 444

Table 1. Weapon Transfers Reported to the
United Nations Register of Conventional Arms

	t Tanks	Armoure d Combat Vehicles	Large Calibre Artillery	Combat Aircraft	Attack Helicopters	Ships	Missiles/ Missile Launchers
Germany	140	136	449	18	1	19	13540
Total	1733	1639	1682	270	40	40	67878

Source: E. Laurance, S. Wezeman, H. Wulf, SIPRI, Arms Watch. SIPRI Report on the
First Year of the UN Register of Conventional Arms, SIPRI Research Report No. 6

The pattern of recipients has changed again recently. The bulk of
exports are now directed at industrialised countries, and within that
group mainly to NATO countries (see figure 1). According to SIPRI, only
one quarter of German have been exported to developing countries during the last five years. While the role of German companies in controversial international deals has attracted much international attention,
the growing importance of Germany as an exporter of major conventional weapons was primarily a domestic issue. Among the major exporters Germany is the only country that has increased its arms sales
during the last five years, thus increasing its share in the shrinking
world market considerably (see figure 2).

The increase in German arms exports has been significantly influenced by the NATO "cascade" of CFE Treaty items, the contribution of
German companies to NATO co-operation projects, the export of ex-
NVA equipment and the cumulation of exports of expensive naval
equipment. The increasing role of Germany as a major arms exporter
was underlined by the United Nations Register of Conventional Arms.
Germany was—behind the United States—the second largest supplier,
with weapons exported in each of the seven weapon categories. Table 1
illustrates this fact.

A particular speciality of German industry, until the early 1980s,
was the sale of production licences and the export of weapon production
facilities. This is a direct result of the restrictive laws. Companies
tried to circumvent the law by exporting production licences and equipment instead of finished weapons. The passing of the new policy guidelines in 1982 was in part a reaction to this trend. Tougher regulations
were applied to the export of production licences.

Exports of civil technology with military significance or application are much more important from an economic perspective than sales
of weapons. The value of goods controlled under the Foreign Trade
Act—which is a proxy for dual-use technology—is several times that
for exports of weapons, as table 2 illustrates.

Table 2. Exports of Weapons and Export Licenses of Sensitive Technology

	value (bn. DM) 1989	value (bn. DM) 1990	value (bn. DM) 1991	value (bn. DM) 1992
Exports of weapons (according to Weapons of War Control Act)	1.54	1.86	4,13	2,63
Value of approved export licences(according to Foreign Trade Act)list A: weapons, munitions and defence material	13.05	5.56	n.a.	9,01
lists: B - E: sensitive technology*	32.47	15.03	n.a.	19,99

Source: Parliamentary enquiry, Deutscher Bundestag, Drucksache 12/1140, 12 Sept. 1991; Parliamentary enquiry, Deutscher Bundestag, Drucksache 12/4794, 27 April 1993; Deutscher Bundestag, Drucksache 12/6585, 11 Jan. 1994, p. 13; communication by the Ministry of Economics to the author 21 Feb. 1994

*Note: * = list B: nuclear material; list C: other goods and technologies of strategic significance; list D: chemical installations; list E: installations for the production of biological substances.*

PRINCIPLE POLICY CHANGE?

The latest policy change began publicly on 1 January 1989 when the *New York Times,* using US intelligence sources, publicised the "Auschwitz in the Dessert" story, uncovering not only illegal German company activity in a chemical weapons factory but, also official German Government knowledge of the deals. Despite the increase in German arms sales, the present policy can be described as more cautious. The changes, mainly a consequence of the Libya and Iraq affairs, go beyond the above described amendments of the law.

German arms export policy has in the past been conspicuously secretive. Parliamentarians and the public at large were usually informed ex post facto, if at all. An annual report, common in several other countries of the West, is absent in Germany. However, after having called many times in the United Nations General Assembly for a United Nations Arms Transfer Register,[12] the Foreign Office made sure that the 1992 Report by Germany was transparent. In contrast to several other major exporters, the German report to the UN contained details on types and models of the exported and imported weapon systems so that a fairly clear picture of 1992 German exports and imports in the UN Register weapon categories is available.

However, doubt is cast on the durability of this change in policy. The German Government has been criticised—this time less so interna-

---

[12] The German Government is among a number of others like Japan, the UK, Italy, that claim parenthood to the UN Register.

tionally than within the country—for exporting numerous weapon systems of the former East German Army (NVA) to a number of countries.
Critics point to the fact—and civil servants in the licensing office privately confirm this view—that an important reason for these exports
was to save the costs that would have been incurred if the weapons
would have been scrapped. Instead of sticking to the newly proclaimed
strict application of restrictive export regulations the Government
opted for exports on economic grounds. Thus, doubt remains if the latest
policy change will be really long lasting.

It is interesting to note that the Government seems sensitive to this
criticism. In its report to the UN it made a special reference to these
transfers by stating: "It becomes obvious from the figures that transfers
mainly took place within NATO and to neighbouring Scandinavia. Deliveries to other countries were rather rare. This reflects German arms
export policy. Recent increases in exports are due to transfers of equipment of the former German Democratic Republic armed forces mainly to
other States parties to the Treaty on Conventional Armed Forces in Europe (CFE). This increase is temporary and does not indicate any
change in the restrictive export policies pursued by the Federal Government."[13]

THE ROLE OF INDUSTRY

German industry is the main—although not the only—driving force
behind less restrictive regulations or controls.[14] Unlike the United
States, Britain, and France, no governmental agency was created to
promote arms exports; this function was left largely to industry. Also,
operating in a public environment that is probably more hostile to-

---

[13] Report of the Secretary General, United Nations Register of Conventional Arms, United
Nations General Assembly, A/48/344, p. 44. Another incident proves the sensitivities of the
German Government. When the 1993 SIPRI Yearbook appeared, the press in Germany
picked up the issue that Germany was number three in arms exports, although this fact is
but a small one page comment in the SIPRI Yearbook. The Government reacted immediately
by stating that the SIPRI figures were based on an "incomprehensible method" and did not
match its own statistics. The differences in the value of weapons exported according to
SIPRI and the Government of Germany (see Figure 1 and table 2) are due to different
methodologies: SIPRI applies its own valuation systems based on production cost; the
German Government records the actual financial transfers of the particulars exports. In
addition SIPRI does not include all equipment (e.g. small arms are excluded) while the
German Government records parts of its defence exports und der Weapons of War Control
Act and other parts are recorded under the Foreign Trade Act.

[14] The sale of NVA equipment from the Army stocks of weapons is not at all in industries
interest. On the contrary in a shrinking market the Government competes with industry.

wards arms exports than in many other countries, German industry was mostly on the defensive.[15]

The arms industry in Germany has gone through several distinct phases.[16] In the early period of the 1950s, after arms production was no longer prohibited, exports did not play an important role. In the early 1960s industry was in a dynamic rebuilding and expansion process and did not depend so much on exports, although tank producers were quite successful in selling the Leopard I tank to several NATO countries and Australia. A first major push for arms exports came during the 1970s when the German arms industry had acquired the whole range of major conventional weapons technology. These efforts were exacerbated during the 1980s both because of favourable Government attitudes as well as emerging excess capacities.

Industry is now faced with a severe crisis. Domestic procurement has been cut and is likely to continue to be reduced. At the same time prospects in exports do not look very promising either. First, because the Government is on a more cautious course as described above and, secondly, and possibly even more important, major recipient countries have reduced their imports due to hard currency constraints.

EUROPEAN VERSUS NATIONAL
EXPORT REGULATIONS

The German Government has declared time and again that it is in favour of harmonised EC-arms export regulations.[17] Realising, however, the differences in the various national laws, a possible compromise of harmonised regulations is controversial in the German public, in Parliament and even within the Government coalition. In a debate in Parliament a conservative CDU/CSU party member, Peter Kittelmann, called for a common European regulation, even at the expense of restrictions in Germany. His colleague from the Liberal party, however, stated that this was an unacceptable proposition and called for keeping strict regulations.[18] In a statement of the foreign policy working group of the CDU/CSU, a consensus is clearly called for

---

[15] It took the arms industry until the 1970s to speak openly about "defence" or "arms" production. In annual reports of the relevant companies arms productions was usually cryptically referred to as "special" production. See Ulrich Albrecht, op cit.

[16] Michael Brzoska, The Federal Republic of Germany, in Nicole Ball and Milton Leitenberg (eds), The Structure of the Defense Industry (Croom Helm: London and Canberra, 1983), pp. 111-139.

[17] For one of the more recent official statements see Deutscher Bundestag, Drucksache 12/4241, 1 Feb. 1993, p. 15.

[18] Deutscher Bundestag, Drucksache 12/5925, 20 Oct. 1993, p. 15746 and p.15747.

in which the German regulations "can not be the only criteria".[19] Their concern is to maintain a viable defence industrial base. In order to keep production facilities occupied they are willing to compromise on export regulations. The Government is inclined to ease the 1982 guidlines and harmonise them with less stringent standards in the European Union. For many with a vested interest, this compromise is a welcome avenue to finally get rid of some of the restrictions in Germany and have harmonised regulations implemented akin to British or French export laws. Under the umbrella of a European law one could even put the blame for aggressive export policies on Brussels.

The crucial question in the present debate is the newly introduced paragraph 5.c (referred to above) of the Foreign Trade Act that regulates dual-use goods and which introduced the catch-all clause. If the present German regulation is not acceptable on a European level—which is very likely—three alternatives remain:

- to accept the future European regulation at the expense of German law (the favourite solution of industry,
- to refuse the European regulation and stick to the new German law, thus, not harmonising European export regulations (the favourite solution of the arms export critics)
- to find a compromise that would call for a revision of the German law by finding a less restrictive paragraph 5.c of the Foreign Trade Act: fewer products, projects and countries than presently would then be on the list (which is the likely outcome).

Harmonisation of exports—from the perspective of German industry—is important to enable them to compete with their West European competitors on equal footing. The decline in procurement orders of the armed forces has led to a variety of company strategies, among them proliferating transnational ties. Major companies tried to improve their business position by increasing their share in a shrinking market at the expense of small and medium size companies. Smaller arms-producing companies were purchased at the national level and cross border mergers and acquisitions occurred at an unprecedented level within the arms industry.[20]

---

[19] Arbeitgruppe Außenpolitik CDU/CSU Fraktion im Deutschen Bundestag, Gemeinsame Europäische Verteidigung, Gemeinsamer Rüstungsmarkt, Gemeinsame Rüstungsexportpolitik, Standortpapiere, Bonn 22 Nov. 1993. This paper has initiated a new debate about the control of dual-use technology that began in January 1994 with senior members of the government pointing out that there is a need to revise the export policy.

[20] Elisabeth Sköns, Western Europe: internationalization of the arms industry, in Herbert Wulf (ed), Arms Industry Limited, (Oxford University Press, Oxford 1993), pp. 160-190.

It seems that for the first time, the 1990s might see the emergence of a truly West European arms industry. A co-ordinated West European approach to weapon development, production, procurement and industry has been requested from different quarters for decades. It has never materialised, despite promises and political action plans. Since the need for adjustment has become apparent, it now seems that industry is prepared to take the necessary action.

For many companies, the route to survival is sought in new co-operation and corporation structures that go beyond the previously well known single programme collaborations (like Panavia of British Aerospace, MBB (DASA) and Alenia to build the Tornado fighter aircraft) or the concentration on families of products (as the previous Westland/Aérospatiale collaboration in helicopters and, more prominently, Airbus civil aircraft production). These traditional types of cross-boundary activity could be seen as "main alliances" to concentrate on major projects.[21] In the 1990s, large West European companies are getting more and more interconnected, not only at the level of joint development or production but also at the capital investment level.[22] The rationale for these company strategies are shrinking markets and tough US competition.

To what extent internationalisation of the large companies has already taken place can be demonstrated by Daimler Benz's subsidiary DASA, the largest German and fourth largest European arms-producing company, which ranks 17th in the SIPRI top 100 list of the world's arms producers.[23] Besides the international connections listed in the table below, DASA has additional foreign investments outside Europe (in the US, Africa and Asia) and in areas such as civil aircraft, space systems, information technology, etc.

---

[21] The term "main alliances" is used and described in great detail particularly for the aerospace sector of the West European arms industry by David Fouquet, Manuel Kohnstamm and Michael Noelke (eds), Dual-Use Industries in Europe, vols. I, II and Executive Summary, Study carried out by Eurostrategies for the Commission of the European Communities, DG III: Brussels, 1991, p. A-81-A-93. For a recent description of the different types of collaborative arrangements see William Walker and Philip Gummett, Nationalism, Internationalism and the European Defence Market, Chaillot Papers 9/September 1993 of the Institute for Security Studies of WEU.

[22] A notable predecessor to the present trend of joint ventures is Euromissile, a company owned by DASA (previously MBB) and Aérospatiale, dating back to 1972, and set up to develop and produce missiles.

[23] This section draws on an unpublished manuscript by Elisabeth Sköns and Herbert Wulf, Internationalisation of the West European Arms Industry, Stockholm/Hamburg Feb. 1994.

Table 3. DASA Foreign Investment in Other European
Arms-Producing Companies (Selection)

Major cooperation partner in joint stock companies	Country	Area	Company/Investment DASA share
Alenia	Italy	fixed wing aircraft	Panavia (42.5%)Eurofighter (33%)
Aérospatiale	France	helicopters	Eurocopter (40%)
Aérospatiale	France	missiles	Euromissile (50%)
British Aerospace	UK	fixed wing aircraft fixed wing aircraft	Panavia (42.5%) Eurofighter (33%)
CASA	Spain	fixed wing aircraft	Eurofighter (33%) and minority shares in CASA (0.7%)
FIAT	Italy	engines engines	Turbo Union (40%) Eurojet Turbo (33%)
Matra	France		Matra MHS (50%)
Rolls-Royce	UK	engines	Turbo Union (40%) Eurojet Turbo (33%)
SENER	Spain	engines	Eurojet Turbo (33%)
Turbomeca	France	engines	MTU Turbomeca Roll-Royce (33,3%)

Source: DASA Geschäftsbericht 1992 (annual report), pp. 34 and 35; and SIPRI data bank

This does not, however, mean that the companies are co-operation partners in all areas or that a structured and streamlined European industry with Eurocompanies is already in existence. On the contrary, the companies are tough competitors particularly in exports.

German companies operating under more restrictive export regulations are particularly concerned and feel disadvantaged against their competitors, particularly from France and the UK. The idea of a licence-free European arms export zone, in which regulations are only applied when exports outside the European Union take place, has attracted support from these industrialists. Yet even initiatives of the European Parliament and of company managers (like Daimler Benz CEO Edzard Reuter in letters to the EC Commission and to the German Chancellor) and industry associations (like the BDI, the German Industry Association) have failed to lead to a harmonisation of export rules in the EC.[24]

---

[24] In a letter to FRG Chancellor Helmut Kohl and to European Commission President Jacques Delors, Edzard Reuter, the Chief Executive Officer of Daimler Benz, proposed the formation of a European Arms Export Control Authority to devise and implement arms export regulations. Agnès Courades Allebeck, The European Community and arms export regulations, in Ian Anthony, op cit., p. 213.

In the past, the major problem arose out of government-to-government co-production projects. The question was—in the absence of European regulations—whose export laws should be applied? This issue has been largely solved by agreeing to co-production projects (based on government agreement) in which each partner can export within its own legal framework. With increased internationalisation of companies outside of narrow co-production agreements, the core issue is export regulations for the supply of components and technology. Which export rules apply in industry co-operation projects? German industrialists ask that the same rules apply as in government-to-government projects.

Existing export regulations are not a trivial matter rather, for some of the major producers, it is a question of survival. Since it is hardly possible for major West European arms producers to rely exclusively on their home market, export regulations are a key to the future. Thomas Enders of DASA believes that, unless the European Union applies common rules and guidelines for exports, there will never be a truly European arms industry. Even the most advanced 'Eurocompanies` like Eurocopter are likely to be re-nationalised, or at least French dominated, and not only because Aérospatiale's capital share is 60 per cent. As long as the German partner has to cope with more restrictive export regulations while the French partner can rely on strong government support for exports, the German company will be at a disadvantage. In the long run, Thomas Enders fears, the German arms industry could even be reduced to a component supplier and loose its capability as a systems integrator.[25] According to independent analysts, these concerns are not just the usual industry rhetoric and cry for help: "The risk that German industries will become disengaged is a real one. Yet it is hardly conceivable that a strong European defence sector can evolve without German participation, given its greater industrial strengths and resources."[26]

---

[25] Phone interview of the author 6 August 1993.

[26] William Walker and Philip Gummett, op. cit. p. 66.

CHAPTER 3

FRENCH ARMS TRADE AND THE EC

Yves Boyer
Deputy Director,
CREST Ecole Polytechnique, Paris

In the 1990s an understanding of the restructuring of the defence industries in a country such as France cannot be fully appreciated if it is not put into historical terms. Traditionally, in France, the State has always played a central role in this field. Back to the late 17th century, Colbert during the reign of Louis the XIVth, was the first to organize, rationalize and develop arsenals to provide, in quantity, weapons of quality for the King's army and navy. This tradition of high involvement of the State has been perpetuated since that time. It should be noted that today, the brightest and the most talented young French men and women who specialize in science compete fiercely to enter *Ecole polytechnique* as this opens the doors to the upper reaches of the industry and banking system. Each year, a substantial numbers of graduates of *Ecole polytechnique*, the *polytechniciens*, are selected for the *Corps de l'armement* which is the ruling elite of the whole French defense armament system in the public and, to a large extent, even in the private sector since a substantial number of *Ingénieurs de l'armement*, in the midst of their career decide to enter the private sector. This historical and sociological factor has to be recalled since it represents a key parameter to understanding French attitudes when dealing with defence industries and the role that may be played in the future by European institutions. This class of leaders be willing to "Europeanize" their practices and the firms in which they operate only if they find that a kind of "European patriotism" does exist guaranteeing that their interests, will be preserved and defended especially vis à vis competitors outside Europe.

In the framework the close connection between the French State and defence industries, promoting French weapons abroad has always been considered good for the country for economic and non economic reasons. This goal has never been questioned by the general population. Accordingly, on the issue of arms trade, there is neither a sense of moral guilt nor heated debates amongst the public of the kind that exists in other West European nations. Selling French weapons abroad has always been traditionally considered as a national goal.

If the Second World War did inflict a severe blow to French defence industries, their reconstruction and renovation under the Fourth Republic (1945-1958) and their rise since the beginning of the Fifth Republic (1958-) stemmed from the conjunction of various factors and particularly the development of an ambitious civilian-military R&D effort. This endeavour favoured leading industries and was speeded up at the beginning of the 60's when the development of a nuclear arsenal by Paris led to the acquisition of many new high-technologies, many of them having a dual application, military and civilian. Such rise was planned by various Defence program laws which offered a financial framework (not always respected), which contributed to develop high-tech industries particularly in the nuclear, aerospace and electronic fields.

Initially oriented to give satisfy national requirements (the national market represented in 1993, a little less than 75% of the national production), French defence industries looked for export at the beginning of the 70's. In 1967, the arms exports represented 5% of the total output of this sector[1] twenty years later this percentage has been increased by 6 to reach 31%[2]. This evolution has been favoured by the State which is represented in this domain by a key player the DGA (*Délégation Générale pour l'Armement*) .

The French State is intervenes in the process of arms export by way of a set of regulations. As a mater of principle, the law prohibits the export of weapons. However, the State retains the right to authorize such sales, on a case by case, basis. The authorization is a complex process. The canvassing of a potential customer is based on an agreement given by an interministerial Commission, the CIEEMG (*Commission Interministérielle pour l'Etude des Exportations de Matériels de Guerre*)[3] which is chaired by the *Secrétaire Général de la Défense Nationale* (SGDN), subordinate to the Prime Minister. In the CIEEMG, there are representatives of the Foreign Affairs, Defence, Interior, Economy and Treasury ministries. Each month, up until the early 1990's, about 600

---

[1] Jacques Isnard, "La fin des marchands de canon", *Le Monde*, 26 June 1990.

[2] In 1990, the production of French defence industries amounted to 124,5 billions FF (2,3% of the GNP) of which, the exports amounted to 38,6 Bn FF.

[3] The CIEEMG has been created by a decree in June 10, 1949.

cases were settled. There are about 4% refusals per year. The reasons to agree or to refuse are various. Among the criteria which are taken into account, there is of course a diplomatic element. In agreeing to sell weapons, France is expressing its support to a friendly country in a given international context which may, of course, fluctuate on a certain period of time. This criteria is particularly noticeable in certain areas where French interests are significant : Europe, the Mediterranean Basin, the Middle-East and Africa. The second imperative debated in the CIEEMG is that, similarly to other arms export countries, France seeks to derive economic benefits. Selling military equipment to foreign countries contributes to the positive side of the balance of payments and reduces in relative terms the costs of military equipment for the French forces. Soon after the selling of Leclerc tanks to Abu Dhabi, in early 1993, the Defence Minister at that time, M. Pierre Joxe, declared that this contract resulted in half a billion of French francs for the MoD budget since the increased number of tanks produced will be translated into an economy of scale with a correlative diminution of costs per unit[4].

The French States is also strongly represented in defence industries since it exercises a powerful control on all the weapons programs through the action of the DGA. Created under the name of *Délégation Ministérielle pour l'Armement* on April 5, 1963, DGA took its current denomination on February 5, 1977.

As part of the Ministry of Defence, the DGA, is in charge of weapons development and production. It also provides long term orientations for this sector of activities at the request of the defence Minister. DGA employs about 53000 peoples in 53 different locations and managed, in 1991, a budget of 100 Bn FF of which 30 were devoted to R&D. The sole research aspect represented in 1992, 7% of the defence equipment budget of the French MoD, i.e. as much as the combined amount spent by the UK and Germany but ten times less than in the USA.

With the nomination of a new head of DGA, Henri Conze, soon after the Balladur Government came into power in the Spring of 1993, it was decided to reform the DGA to take into account the transformations of the geostrategic scene, the fact that France's defence industries were in excess of capacity as well as the necessity to cope with a new phase in the technological competition at the world level[5].

The French State is also a key player in the evolution of the defence industrial sector since it exercises direct and indirect control on the major firms involved in this area. For a very long period of time,

---

4 Pierre Joxe, interview, *Les Echos*, March 2, 1993.
5The plan to reshuffle the DGA were made public by H. Conze in October 19, 1993. See Info-DGA 1/94.

the State directly controlled and indeed even owned huge part of the industry but, since the late 1980's there has been a movement towards disengagement in terms of ownership. The last move in that direction has been the vote by the Parliament, in the Spring of 1993, of a law authorizing the privatization of major firms like Thomson, Aérospatiale and SNECMA. The defence industries sector is indeed of a paramount importance for the industrial life of the country : it represents roughly 7% of the industrial activities in France. It amounted, on average since the 1980's, to 4% of the French exports as a whole. This is also a very high added value sector : 30% of the funds of the MoD equipment budget is devoted to R&D. In total, the defence industries represent 18% of the national efforts for research;a significant effort in R&D. In defence electronics industries 52% of the R&D is financed by the firms themselves, 20 to 35% in aerospace industries. This is a relatively huge effort which contributes to explain that France high-tech industries have been strengthened since the early 80's.

Another characteristic of this sector that is that it is highly concentrated : 13 main contractors with the French MoD represent 80% of the total financial output of this sector and 90% of the defence programs. Among those firms, one finds : Thomson-CSF, Aérospatiale, DCN, GIAT Industries, Dassault Aviation and Matra. At the same time, paradoxically, the industrial activities are very diffuse since more than 5000 firms contributed in 1993 to this sector. It became recently a high priorty for DGA to help, despite the reduction of the defence industries sector, small or medium size firms which are highly specialized and posssessing a specific technological know-how to remain in business. A specific program called ASTRID (*Accompagnement structurel des industries de défense*) was initiated in 1993 to guarantee they will be able to reinforce their capital.

In France the ground equipment industries are formed by more than 50 firms regrouped within the framework of a syndicate the GICAT (*Groupement des Industries concernées par les Matériels de Défense Terrestre*). In this sector one finds firms producing:

- vehicles and weapons such as GIAT-Industries[6,] RVI, SNPE, Panhard;
- electronics systems : Thomson-CSF, SAGEM, SAT, SFIM, Dassault Electronique;
- helicopters and their weapons : Aérospatiale and Matra.

---

[6] GIAT Industries has been created on July 1, 1990. It regrouped industrial activities of the *Direction des Armements Terrestres* (DAT) a subdivision of DGA, Manhurin Défense, Luchaire, Herstal and PRB.

The principal firm in this field is GIAT-Industries with a total output of 8,4 Bn FF in 1991 and 12,000 employees.

The financial output in this sector has diminished by 31% since 1990 and the number of employees has decreased during the same period by 28%.

DCN is the prime contractor for naval equipment. In 1992, its financial output was 15,8Bn FF. DCN was reorganized in 1992 with the creation of DCNI (DCN *Industrielle*) which introduced a legal difference between responsibilities of the French State which supervise DCN as a branch of the DGA and the industrial and commercial activities of DCN.

Dassault Aviation is the sole French defence aircraft fighter manufacturer. Its financial output was 17,6 Bn FF in 1988, but this fell to 11,6 Bn FF in 1993. Dassault Aviation is part of the Dassault group and employed 21 000 people in 1990. Dassault Aviation employed 10 000 persons in 1993 compared to 17 000 five years earlier. In December 1992, the State transferred its financial participation to SOGEPA (*Société de Gestion et de Participation Aéronautique*). The result was not a merger but rather a tutelage of both firms by a holding belonging to the State. SOGEPA will coordinate the actions of both companies (its shares in Dassault's capital is 35% and 20% in the case of Aérospatiale) particularly when they deal with their European counterparts, DASA and British Aerospace.

Thomson-CSF have, in 1992, a financial output of 35 Bn of FF of which 25,7 Bn FF are from its armament sector. This is the largest European defence electronic firms and the second at the world level behind Hughes. Its activities are highly dependent from the defence sector as well as the export market (60% of its total activities). In six years from 1987 to 1993 the number of its employees fell from 44,500 to 34,000.

MATRA Défense Espace is specialized in the production of certain type of missiles (air to air and air to ground) and in satellites. Its current activities are based on the sales of three missiles, the short-range SAM Mistral, the Mica air to air missile, the sole West European competitor to the US AMRAAM, and the air to ground Apache missile.

THE CURRENT SITUATION OF FRENCH DEFENCE INDUSTRIES AND THE EXPORT OF WEAPONS

Since the early 1990's French defence industries, similarly to their counterparts in the Western world, have suffered a difficult period of adaptation to a new landscape characterized by a cumulative decrease of the internal and external markets. Various indicators have caused this crisis. The slow down of the defence effort in the Western world have been translated into the diminution of the equipment budget. In the UK the equipment spending in 1993 was 41% below those of 1983; in Germany the percentage is even higher (60%); in the USA the level remain constant between those two dates. In France, the equipment spending has decreased by 6% in real terms between 1990 and 1993 (see chart below). The total financial output of the defence industries sector was 113 Bn FF in 1992, a diminution of 5% in constant FF with 1991. This amount represented 2% of the total industrial production in France. The arms export market has also diminished and represented in 1993, 4% of French exports. Its financial output has decreased by 19% for France between 1984 (56,4 Bn FF) and 1992 (48 Bn FF). The same is true for Western Europe with 10,5 Bn Ecu of weapons export in 1992 against 17,4 in 1984.

This reduction of the production has had severe consequences on the employment in the defence industrial sector. In 1993, the number of direct employees was 230,000 (slightly more than 1% of the total active population) of which 189,000 were employed for national purposes and 41 000 for export[7]. In addition, more than 100,000 persons are also indirectly employed in this sector. These figures are a decrease from previous years. In the aerospace industries, the financial output has decreased by 10% from 1990 to 1993 and correlatively the number of employees has diminished from 120,719 persons to 105 300[8]. To avoid a further diminution, short time working has been adopted representing 4% of the working time, the equivalent of 4,600 jobs. Despite these adjustments, it is anticipated in the next five years a further reduction of about 20,000 to 75,000 people[9] will take place. This reduction may affect more deeply some areas than others since, in four regions, the activities in defence industries involve more than 10% of the economically active population (Aquitaine, Ile-de- France, Provence-Côte d'Azur, Bretagne), in some departments, the percentage is even above 20% (Var, Cher, Hautes Pyrénées and Finistère)[10] As a whole, the French Defence industries are in a relative state of crisis. Various factors do explain this situation : a global excess in capacity, the limitation of the market on a national base, and a decrease in the export of weapons. Such a deep crisis may increase the danger that the United States will benefit to the detriment of the European Union. In global terms the EU and the USA have the same share of world industrial

---

[7] See : L'Avenir des Industries Liées à la Défense, Groupe des Stratégie Industrielle, Chaired by Marcel Bénichou. Commissariat Général du Plan, nov. 1993, *La Documentation Française*.

[8] "Les industriels de l'armement croient à une reprise économique à partir de 1995"; *Les Echos*, April 21, 1994.

[9] Bénichou op. cit.

[10] "La crise des industries de défense", Assemblée Nationale, Commission de la Défense, Rapport d'information, October 5, 1993; by René Galy-Dejean.

production, about 20% each, but if one looks at the financial output of US and EU defence firms the imbalance is striking. In 1993, the US firms represented 32% of the world financial output of defence industries against 14% for the EU firms in that sector[11]. In the 1994's annual ranking of the top 100 defence contractors worldwide on the basis of annual defence sales, one find among the first 50, 32 US firms and only 13 European (7 French, 3 British and 1 for Germany, Italy and Sweden)[12]. Such an imbalance between the two sides of the Atlantic may increase in the future since as a whole the United States is devoting far more investments into R&D. In 1992, the USA invested 27,4 Bn Ecu in military R&D, France 5,2, the UK 3,79 and Germany 1,23.

The defence program law debated by the French Parliament in the spring of 1994 may bring some relief to the defence industry. This law which covers the 1995-2000 period plans a moderate increase in real terms of the defence spending devoted to equipment (0.5% per year in constant FF). From 1994 to 2000, 613.1Bn FF(1994 value) will be spent on equipment. This obviously reassured the heads of defence industries since it provides them with a relatively assured framework which dissipates many uncertainties and allow them to plan their activities. In addition no big defence programs has been either canceled or dramatically curtailed (Rafale aircraft, Leclerc MBT, nuclear aircraft carrier, NH-90 transport helicopter, M4/M5 SLBM's, etc...). However if everything is preserved in the short term, one shall add that the law remain indicative. Nothing guarantee that in two or three years from now the plan cannot be reviewed and diminished.

TOWARDS THE EUROPEANIZATION OF DEFENCE INDUSTRIES

Various reasons have militated against the development of a greater integration between West European defence industries. Important among them has been the imperative of survival vis a vis American competitors which possesses a far greater internal market and benefits indirectly from the huge defence budget of the Pentagon which is four time greater than those combined of Britain, Germany and France in 1992[13]. The US arms export are also vigorously supported politically,

---

[11] Rapport Galy-Dejean op. cit."La crise des industries de défense", Assemblée Nationale, Commission de le Défense, Rapport d'information, October 5, 1993; By René Galy-Dejean.

[12] Defense News Top 100, *Defense News*, July 18-24, 1994.

[13] Military Balance 1993-1994, the IISS.

diplomatically and economically by the US authorities at the highest level[14].

In Europe the political framework does exist for such an evolution. The Petersburg declaration of June 19, 1992, from WEU, following what was agreed in the Maastricht conference, provided general guidelines to deepen cooperation within the EU in the field of defence industries. An evolution has already begun with, for example the devolution of the former IEPG activities to the WEU and the setting up of West European Armament Group (WEAG) and the creation of a European Armament Agency. France and Germany having expressed their will to go faster than their other partners and created a Franco-German Armament Agency in 1995. The WEAG may become the vehicle for European preferential purchase of weapons, even if it seems doubtful that agreement will be reached with all the EC members.

In France there has been clearly a shift in priorities as expressed by the *Livre Blanc* on defence published in February 1994. In many fields, including defence industries there will be a voluntary policy deepening cooperation at the EU level. This "europeanization" will go along with a rationalization of European defence industries. On the demand side, European structures such as the future Armament Agency should play a leading role; on the supply side there will be a restructuring of European industries with the emphasis on major West European firms.[15]. In a more concrete terms there are already a variety of action being undertaken which may gradually create better synergistic effects at the level of West European defence industries.

1. In the major countries of the EU, a greater share of the R&D will be devoted to co-operative programs. In France for example, in 1984, 5% of the military R&D investments was devoted to cooperation with European partners, eight years later the share reached 23%[16]. In this field it may be advisable to develop at the European level multinational R&D organizations on the model of the Franco-German institute of Saint-Louis. In the fierce competition in the field of high-tech this is particularly important. In the mid 80's, the development of a new technology in the field of electronic component represented a cost of about $100 million, in 1993, the cost was about one billion $[17]. The significant increase cost of the defence R&D is reinforcing the trend towards industrial concentration to acquire a serial effect. Such concen-

---

[14] On that issue, see : "Rapport relatif à la programmation militaire pour les années 1995 à 2003", Jacques Genton, Commission des Affaires étrangères, de la défense et des forces armées, Sénat, June 8, 1994.

[15] The defence Minister F. Léotard developped those ideas in a speech made when opening the 30th session of the Centre des Hautes Études de l'Armement, september 8, 1993, Paris.

[16] Rapport Bénichou op. cit.

[17] "La politique militaire de la France et son financement", Assemblée Nationale, Commission de l'Economie générale et du Plan, July 2, 1993. Report by Arthur Paecht and Patrick Balkany.

tration has not yet been fully undertaken in the defence industrial sector for reasons of national independence. However for the survival of the European defence industry it must be done at the European level.

2. The rapid integration and rapprochement amongst West European defence industrial groups is needed in order to compete more efficiently on the world arena with US defence companies. These continue to overwhelm the European firms both in terms of R&D resources and in terms of economy of scale with an internal market far greater than any single national market in Western Europe. In juridical terms it may be necessary to go beyond the legal status of GIE (*Groupement d'Intérêt Economique*) and enable various European defence industries to pool resources in common to develop specific products such as Euromissile which specializes in anti-tank missiles. Indeed, the GIE formula has been the juridical consequence of the refusal by European countries to select on a transnational base the most efficient firms for military equipment. In the future it is a necessity to go beyond the GIE formula in favouring the multinational merger of activities at the European level. Regarding the current West European redundant capacities in defence industries and the imperatives to develop cooperation far beyond the stage of production, the GIE formula is insufficient. The solution may be found in financial merger, the big national companies having together the same subsidiaries. This is already the case with the creation of Eurocopter which has resulted from the merger of the helicopter divisions of Aérospatiale and Deutsche Aerospace. In July 1994 it was announced that there would be a regrouping between subsidiaries of Thomson-CSF and DASA in the field of propulsion and ammunition, with a total output of 1.4Bn FF[18.] This was also the case with the creation by Matra and GEC of Matra Marconi Space. This movement shall, of course go along with the development of a kind of "buy European" attitude. Such *préférence communautaire* will only with difficulty be accepted by the small countries of the EU and by the United Kingdom whose tendency is to look first towards the United States. The attitude of London vis à vis the replacement for the RAF of the aging Hercules transport airplane will be a very good test of the real desire of the British with regard to the development of a European aerospace and defence industries. There is no doubt that a renunciation of the European FLA project by the UK will represent another severe blow to the capacity of the EU to cope efficiently with US defence and aerospace firms.

3. The way in which the European Commission conceives its industrial policy may have to be reconsidered. In the defence and aerospace industrial sectors intra-European criteria relating to mergers and acqui-

---

[18] "Défense: l''alliance avec les allemands sème le trouble"; *La Tribune Desfossés*, July 7, 1994. The subsidiaries are Thomson Brandt Armement and Wirksysteme.

sitions should not apply when related to acquisition outside the EU. They should be replaced by criteria based on global competition. In this field the De Haviland fiasco, where Aerospatiale and Alenia, associated in the GIE ATR were prevented from acquiring De Haviland-Canada left a bitter taste amongst France's aerospace and defence community. Vis à vis the external world, the need of protecting European defence industries is widely spread in France. The basic idea is to closely copy what has been done in the US with the Exxon-Florio legislation. The US legislation is particularly protective against foreign acquisitions. This was experienced by the French when Thomson tried to acquire Martin Marieta. When it comes to the restructuring of the European defence industries should not apply free market rules. Certainly, the EC/s main competitor in this field does not do so. MATRA's difficulties with its American subsidiary Fairchild should be noted in this regard.

CONCLUSION

To many French observers it seems premature to be already setting up specific rules regarding arms export when the main objective of promoting arms sales to the best interest of the EU, and the restructuring of its defence industries are not yet concluded. It is now clearly acknowledged in France that, with very few exceptions, it is no longer possible to maintain independence in every sectors of the defence industry. Accordingly, the development of West European joint ventures should be favoured as well as the opening of the European defence market. At the same time a hardened position vis à vis the US protectionist measures[19] should be contemplated on the model of what is done in the United States. Before harmonizing arms trade procedures, the West European have to make their defence industries capable of surviving very harsh competition at the international level. This should be a priority task of the WEU and its future armament agency. The EC should go along with this process. As in other domains, the spirit in which the restructuring will be thought of will reveal the main ideological trend underlying European integration. Will it be accomplished as if the EU is only a free market zone ? Or will the restructuring be undertaken with the view that the EC will gradually become a real community, a zone of intimate solidarity amongs its members? The answer that will emerge will deeply influence French attitudes in the field of defence industries as well as in many other aspects of the European construction.

---

19 See Rapport Bénichou op. cit.

CHAPTER 4

DEVOLUTION OF THE NONPROLIFERATION REGIME?

UNITED STATES AND EUROPEAN EXPORT CONTROL POLICIES IN THE POST COLD WAR ERA

Zachary S. Davis
Congressional Research Service[1]

The United States has been battling proliferation for over fifty years. Beginning with the secrecy that surrounded the Manhattan Project, United States nonproliferation policy has kept a close guard on information, technology, and materials that could assist other nations to build weapons of mass destruction. Even America's Manhattan Project partners Great Britain and Canada were shut out of the U.S. nuclear program to prevent the spread of nuclear know-how. Over nearly five decades, most nations have joined an international consensus against the proliferation of weapons of mass destruction. Nuclear, chemical, and biological weapons and missiles are particularly destabilizing because they can cause abrupt changes in regional distributions of power. Thus, controlling them has taken precedence over efforts to control transfers of conventional weaponry. As the nonproliferation consensus expanded, so did the nonproliferation regime.

The nonproliferation consensus is growing, spurred in part by lessons learned from Iraq's nuclear, chemical, biological and missile programs. However, one major component of nonproliferation policy -- export controls -- may not keep pace with the proliferation threat. Despite recent advances in multilateral cooperation to control exports of technology

---

[1] The views expressed are the authors' and do not necessary reflect the views of the Congressional Research Service or the Library of Congress.

that could contribute to weapons development, United States and European nonproliferation export controls are being challenged. A significant liberalization of controls on dual-use technology could increase proliferation dangers and seriously harm the nonproliferation regime.

THE EVOLUTION OF NONPROLIFERATION EXPORT CONTROLS

Preventing the spread of nuclear weapons ranks as the top nonproliferation priority. This is due to the far greater destructive potential of even a crude (first generation) or small (low yield) nuclear device when compared to known chemical or biological weapons.[2] Thus, nuclear export controls have been the spearhead of the nonproliferation regime. The secrecy and complete denial of the Manhattan Project and the early postwar years gave way to policies to establish guidelines for international commerce in nuclear materials and technology. President Eisenhower's Atoms for Peace proposal and the 1954 Atomic Energy Act established new norms for nuclear transfers, including the application of safeguards on nuclear exports. Controls applied initially to nuclear materials, complete reactors, and information. As recognition of the proliferation threat grew, so did national lists of controlled exports to include a wider range of nuclear technology such as uranium enrichment and plutonium extraction (reprocessessing) technology. International agreements codified the norms and institutions of the nonproliferation regime. Article I of the 1968 Nuclear Nonproliferation Treaty (NPT) is explicit on the commitment of nuclear weapon states:

> ...not to transfer to any recipient whatsoever nuclear weapons or other nuclear explosive devices or control over such weapons or explosive devices directly, or indirectly; and *not in any way* to assist, encourage, or induce any non nuclear weapon State to manufacture or otherwise acquire nuclear weapons or other nuclear explosive devices, or control over such weapons or explosive devices.

The Indian nuclear test in 1974 inspired the United States and others to strengthen their export control policies. The Nuclear Nonproliferation Act of 1978 established new criteria for U.S. nuclear cooperation, including a precedent-setting requirement of full scope International Atomic Energy Agency (IAEA) safeguards on all nuclear activi-

---

[2] Office of Technology Assessment, *Proliferation of Weapons of Mass Destruction, Assessing the Risks* (Washington: U.S. Government Printing Office, 1993) p. 52. Developments in biological weapons could eventually warrant a reevaluation of this assessment.

ties (in any non-nuclear weapon state) as a condition of export.[3] This law required the President to establish controls "over all export items...which could be, if used for the purposes other than those for which the export is intended, of significance for nuclear explosive purposes."[4] Moreover, the Export Administration Act of 1979 established a code of nuclear export regulations and procedures for reviewing export license applications for nuclear related dual-use technology. Congress also amended the Foreign Assistance Act to stop U.S. assistance to countries which violate their nonproliferation commitments.[5] The Carter administration also launched a controversial policy to end the use of plutonium fuels worldwide.

Several European nations rejected initially U.S. efforts to restrict nuclear exports, instead insisting on their rights to export nuclear technology. Thus, Germany and France took the lead in transferring unsafeguarded nuclear technology to nations such as India, Pakistan, China, Israel, Iran, Iraq, Argentina, Brazil, and other countries.[6] France refused to join the NPT. The Europeans nevertheless agreed to establish guidelines for voluntary cooperation in nuclear export controls. The Nuclear Suppliers Group (NSG), first known as the London Club, met in 1975 to discuss adopting a common policy on nuclear transfers. In 1977 the NSG endorsed a set of "Guidelines on Nuclear Transfers."[7] The NSG guidelines advanced the export control standards set by the NPT, but progress stopped at that point.[8] The group did not meet again until March 1991 -- after the war with Iraq. By that time, however, the weaknesses of the voluntary guidelines were apparent.

SAFEGUARDS

Safeguards evolved in tandem with export controls to assure that exports of civilian nuclear technology would not be diverted for military purposes. The International Atomic Energy Agency administered the nuclear bargain, including the requirement of safeguards on nuclear

---

[3] Full scope safeguards require that recipient nations allow IAEA safeguards on all nuclear activities anywhere in the country. Less stringent safeguards are limited to the specific application or project for which imported technology is used.

[4] Nuclear Nonproliferation Act of 1978, P.L. 95-242, section 309(c).

[5] Zachary S. Davis, *Nonproliferation Regimes, Policies to Control the Spread of Nuclear, Chemical and Biological Weapons and Missiles* (Washington DC: Congressional Research Service, 1993).

[6] European transfers of nuclear technology are documented in Leonard Spector's series of books from 1984 through his latest, *Nuclear Ambitions* (Boulder: Westview, 1990).

[7] The IAEA published the NSG guidelines as IAEA document INFCIRC/254, 1978.

[8] See Tadeusz Strulak, "The Nuclear Suppliers Group," The Nonproliferation Review, Fall 1993, vol. 1, no. 1.

transfers.[9] Initially, safeguards were arranged on a bilateral or multi-lateral basis (as in EURATOM), but the NPT advanced safeguards by requiring each non nuclear weapon signatory of the treaty to negotiate a safeguards agreement with the IAEA. Although many countries initially resisted the full scope safeguards requirement, it has become an accepted norm of international nuclear commerce. However, the weaknesses of IAEA safeguards, particularly regarding undeclared activities, have been demonstrated in the Iraq and North Korea cases.

NONPROLIFERATION IN THE POST COLD WAR ERA: ADVANCE OR RETREAT?

Will proliferation accelerate or fade away? The United Nations Security Council, NATO, the European Commission, the G-7, and the individual governments belonging to these organizations have identified the proliferation of weapons of mass destruction to be a major threat to world peace and security. So far, the end of bipolarity seems to be characterized by increased regional conflict rather than ushering in an era of peace and stability. If the security of nations is threatened, and no superpower is willing (or able) to extend credible security guarantees, the result could be a surge of interest in nuclear, chemical and biological weapons and missiles.[10] Thus, the post Cold War era could see an escalation of the proliferation threat.

Many governments are taking steps to address this threat. After the war with Iraq, the Bush administration stepped up U.S. nonproliferation efforts with its Enhanced Proliferation Control Initiative. The Clinton administration unveiled its nonproliferation policy in September 1993, and is undertaking major reorganizations of the Departments of State, Defense, Energy, and the Arms Control and Disarmament Agency to reflect the higher priority of nonproliferation in U.S. foreign policy.[11] Congress has passed several new laws to strengthen U.S. nonproliferation policy.[12] Other countries -- notably Germany -- are also re-

---

[9] On the history of the International Atomic Energy Agency and its safeguards system see Lawrence Scheinman, The International Atomic Energy Agency and World Nuclear Order (Washington DC: Resources for the Future, 1987).

[10] Benjamin Frankel argues that the end of the Cold War will result in many nations, some of whom have foresworn any interest in nuclear weapons, revisiting their nuclear options. See Benjamin Frankel, "The Brooding Shadow: Systemic Incentives and Nuclear Weapons Proliferation," in Zachary Davis and Benjamin Frankel, eds., The Proliferation Puzzle, Why Nuclear Weapons Spread and What Results (London: Frank Cass, 1993).

[11] White House Fact Sheet, Nonproliferation and Export Control Policy, September 27, 1993.

[12] Zachary S. Davis, Nuclear Nonproliferation Issues in the 103rd Congress (Washington: Congressional Research Service, 1993)

organizing bureaucracies and passing new laws to improve the implementation of nonproliferation commitments.[13] Perhaps motivated by scandals over German exports to Iraq and elsewhere, in 1990 Germany adopted a full scope safeguards policy.

In addition to national efforts to strengthen controls on sensitive exports, the United States and its allies have reinvigorated multilateral export control regimes to close loopholes that enabled Iraq and others to build weapons of mass destruction. The Nuclear Suppliers Group met in 1991 for the first time in thirteen years to review and expand its list of sensitive items as well as its membership. A year of negotiations produced a new nuclear control list and a new set of guidelines and procedures for transfers of nuclear-related dual-use commodities. The NSG, now expanded to 28 countries, also declared a joint policy of requiring full scope safeguards on all nuclear exports to non-nuclear weapon states.[14] These changes reflect a shared perception of increased proliferation dangers and represent a major advance in the nonproliferation regime.

Progress is also evident in the chemical and missile nonproliferation regimes. U.S.-Soviet bilateral agreements to dismantle all chemical weapons and the expansion of the Australia Group's list of controlled chemicals were a prelude to the conclusion of the global Chemical Weapons Convention in 1993. Also in 1993, the Missile Technology Control Regime expanded its membership and the scope of its restrictions on transfers of missile technology.[15]

Members of the international community took other steps to strengthen the nonproliferation regime after the war with Iraq. United Nations Security Council Resolution 687, which ended the war, created a Special Commission with extraordinary powers to find and eliminate Iraq's weapons of mass destruction. Resolution 687 gave the IAEA an opportunity to find and destroy the clandestine nuclear program that it failed to detect during years of regular inspections. The success of the Special Commission and the IAEA in carrying out the mandate of the Security Council gave rise to expectations about future international enforcement of nonproliferation commitments. Might Special Commissions be useful elsewhere? Should the Security Council establish a permanent body to enforce nonproliferation commitments?

---

[13] Harald Muller, editor, European Nonproliferation Policy 1988-1992 (Brussels: European Interuniversity Press, 1993); and Bernd Kubbig, German and American Export Control Policies in an Era of Proliferation: From Divergence to Convergence? (Kingston, Ontario: Centre for International Relations, 1993).

[14] INFCIRC/405, May 1992, Statement on Full Scope Safeguards Adopted by the Adherents to the Nuclear Suppliers Guidelines; INFCIRC/254/Rev.1/Part 2, July 1992, Communications Received from Certain Member States Regarding Guidelines for the Export of Nuclear Material, Equipment and Technology, Nuclear-related Dual-use Transfers.

[15] U.S. Department of State, Dispatch, volume 4, number 3, March 1993, p.41.

The discovery of Iraq's nuclear program inspired new efforts to strengthen the IAEA. IAEA officials took the lead in outlining the lessons of Iraq:

- the agency depends on its members for information about undeclared activities. IAEA can use intelligence information provided by member countries, as it did to under Resolution 687 in Iraq.
- the agency lacks sufficient resources to expand the scope and effectiveness of its safeguards system. With a budget of about $60 million, IAEA barely maintains its current responsibilities; new missions require additional support.
- the agency has, but had not previously asserted, authority to conduct special inspections and to inspect all nuclear activities in all non-weapon NPT states.
- the agency depends on its members acting through the Board of Governors to assure access for inspections. If access is denied, its only recourse is to report that it cannot verify compliance with safeguards. It is up to the Board to direct the Director General to report noncompliance to the Security Council.
- it is up to the Security Council to authorize enforcement actions, including sanctions or the use of force.

IAEA applied the lessons of Iraq when it discovered North Korea's noncompliance with its safeguards agreement. IAEA used intelligence information and asserted its full inspection authority to determine that North Korea had not declared a number of significant materials and facilities. It could not, however, assure its access to undeclared sites. Pyongyang's flaunting of its NPT obligations further highlighted the limitations of treaties and international organizations to enforce nonproliferation commitments. Nevertheless, IAEA remains the cornerstone of international cooperation to deter and detect violations of nonproliferation commitments.

Finally, the European Community (EC) exhibited a renewed commitment to nonproliferation. One indication of EC support for strengthening the nonproliferation regime is that the Maastricht Treaty includes nonproliferation as a top priority for unified EC action.[16] Furthermore, beginning in 1990 the EC declared its support for the NPT, strengthening the IAEA, and the NSG. The members have gradually

---

[16] On EC nonproliferation policy see Julien Goens and Alain Michel, "The European Community," in Muller, *op cit.*

harmonized their export control lists, although some problems apparently remain.[17]

These positive developments that strengthened the nonproliferation regime are counter-balanced by other developments that either weaken the regime or create new proliferation hazards. Looking at the positive and negative developments, the question arises whether efforts to maintain the regime are keeping pace with proliferation.

While the established technology suppliers have made progress in their efforts to block the efforts of proliferators to acquire sensitive technology, new suppliers provide alternative sources of supply to nations that do not accept the norms of commerce in nuclear, chemical, and missile technology. A few countries that are capable of exporting nuclear and other advanced technology are not members of the NSG and do not require full scope safeguards. This problem diminished with the expansion of the NSG and MTCR membership, but a few suppliers are still not members. China is probably the most important non-NSG supplier, and its continuing nuclear assistance to Pakistan, Iran, and others is a major nonproliferation problem. [18] China's commitment to uphold the MTCR guidelines is also highly controversial. Other potential new suppliers include India, Pakistan, Iran, Iraq, North Korea, and several of the Soviet successor states. The former Soviet Union could be the greatest proliferation danger today.[19]

New suppliers are not the only problem; recent efforts to strengthen export controls may not be enough to prevent traditional suppliers in the West from contributing to proliferation. In fact, there are signs of deterioration in various parts of the regime. For example, one of the most effective nonproliferation institutions may be on the verge of extinction. The Coordinating Committee for Multilateral Export Controls, known as COCOM, is being abandoned because its primary purpose was to restrict technology transfers to Communist bloc nations. Despite ongoing concerns about illicit transfers to, from, and through Eastern Europe

---

[17] See Harald Muller, "Europe's Leaky Borders," *Bulletin of the Atomic Scientists*, June 1993, p. 27.

[18] Zachary Davis and Shirley Kan, "China's Nonproliferation Policy and Behavior: Challenges for the United States," in Mitchell Reiss, ed., *Nuclear Proliferation in the 1990s* (Baltimore: Johns Hopkins University, forthcoming).

[19] On the potential for nuclear proliferation from the former Soviet Union see: William Potter, *Nuclear Profiles of the Soviet Successor States* (Monterey: Monterey Institute of International Studies, 1993); Kurt Campbell, Ashton Carter, Steven Miller, Charles Zraket, *Soviet Nuclear Fission, Control of the Nuclear Arsenal in a Disintegrating Soviet Union* (Cambridge: Harvard University, 1991); Zachary Davis, Jonathan Medalia, *Nuclear Proliferation from Russia: Options for Control* (Washington: Congressional Research Service, 1992).

and the former Soviet Union, COCOM has been branded as a Cold War relic and is slated for dismantlement.[20]

The establishment of an EC common market could also cause problems for nonproliferation, despite recent efforts to firm up EC export control policy. Any EC export control policy is only as strong as its weakest link. If sensitive items are allowed to circulate freely without controls within the EC, proliferators are likely to target the EC members with the weakest border controls as possible access points for the items they seek. Using sophisticated procurement networks, they may launch elaborate schemes to conceal the identities of actual end users, perhaps using countries such as Greece or Portugal as trans shipment points. As implementation and enforcement of EC export controls is still the responsibility of the members, it remains to be seen if the Maastricht Treaty will advance or retard the cause of nonproliferation.

The nuclear suppliers are not the only ones to apply the lessons of Iraq; proliferators have also adjusted their strategies. One outcome of the investigation of Iraq's weapons programs was a wider appreciation for the size and sophistication of Baghdad's procurement operations. The former Soviet Union, China, Pakistan, Israel, Iran, and others have also conducted aggressive campaigns to acquire materials, technology and expertise from the West. Investigations of the BCCI and Banco Lavoro Nationale scandals revealed the important role of international financial transactions for aiding proliferation.[21] Procurement efforts are likely to be more sophisticated and more difficult to detect in the future.[22] At the same time, proliferators have accumulated considerable knowledge about weapon design and the equipment needed to build nuclear bombs.

Another lesson for nuclear proliferators is that unless the IAEA strengthens its safeguards system and gets more support from its members, it is possible hide a clandestine weapons program, and to block

---

[20] "Will COCOM Have a Successor?" *Intelligence Newsletter*, November 25, 1993; "Administration Warned Against Linking COCOM Reform, Arms Control," *Inside US Trade*, September 17, 1993, p.1.; "Clinton Expected to Scrap Cold War Era Trade Controls," *Washington Times*, September 29, 1993; "House Presses Administration for COCOM Decontrols," *Export Control News*, September 30, 1993.

[21] U.S. Senate, Committee on Banking, Housing, and Urban Affairs, Hearing on U.S. Export Policy Toward Iraq Prior to Iraq's Invasion of Kuwait, October 27, 1992, S.Hrg. 102-996; U.S. House, Committee on Energy and Commerce, Subcommittee on Oversight and Investigations, Hearing on Failed Efforts to Curtail Iraq's Nuclear Weapons Program, April 24, 1991.

[22] On proliferation procurement networks see: U.S. House, Committee on Foreign Relations, Subcommittee on International Security, International Organizations and Human Rights, Hearing on U.S. Security Policy and the "Rogue Regimes" Weapons Acquisition and Supplier Networks, September 14, 1993; Kenneth Katzman, *Iraq's Campaign To Acquire and Develop High Technology* (Washington: Congressional Research Service, 1992); Kenneth Timmerman, *The Death Lobby: How the West Armed Iraq* (New York: Houghton Mifflin, 1991).

access to secret facilities, even if the IAEA asserts its right to inspect undeclared sites. Proliferators may also find better ways to conceal clandestine activities, including underground facilities and ingenious methods of misleading ("spoofing") surveillance efforts. Chemical and biological weapons activities are easier to conceal than nuclear programs. Most disturbing of all may be the precedent set by North Korea when it declared itself not bound by the NPT by virtue of having threatened to leave the treaty. These factors suggest that proliferation is an ongoing challenge.

THE CLINTON NONPROLIFERATION AND EXPORT CONTROL POLICY

Perhaps the most significant indicator of future trends in nonproliferation policy is the Clinton administration's dual use export policy. President Clinton outlined his nonproliferation policy in a speech to the United Nations on September 26, 1993. In his speech the President vowed to make nonproliferation a top priority and to "remove outdated controls that unfairly burden legitimate commerce and unduly restrain growth and opportunity all over the world."[23] The policy, however, appears to go in two opposite directions; one in the direction of expanding the nonproliferation regime and the other in the direction of shrinking it. What developments in the world would warrant a scaling back of export controls? If, as the President observed, "the end of the cold war did not bring us to the millennium of peace," but instead "removed the lid from many cauldrons of ethnic, religious and territorial animosity," then we should expect the causes of proliferation to remain constant or possibly increase. The combination of continuing interest in weapons of mass destruction and deregulation of sensitive exports could increase proliferation risks.

The new U.S. policy could tear the fabric of the nonproliferation regime. By not acknowledging the tension between the contradictory goals of nonproliferation and easing access to sensitive technologies, the policy sends a signal that U.S. leadership in strengthening nonproliferation controls has been suspended. A report by the Commerce Department Trade Promotion Coordinating Committee released in conjunction with the nonproliferation policy spells out the export deregulation policy. A comprehensive review will hold as its objectives to remove unilateral U.S. controls, and to substitute the standard of foreign availability for the traditional nonproliferation criteria found in the

---

[23] Clinton's speech to the United Nations, September 27, 1993, Reuters.

Nonproliferation Treaty and in U.S. laws and regulations.[24] Thus, if others are selling sensitive technology, U.S. exporters will be free to compete.[25] The review also seeks to remove controls on exports to Eastern Europe and the former Soviet Union, reduce the number of export licenses required, streamline the licensing process for all exports, significantly raise the threshold of computing power that can be exported, reduce the referral roles of the Departments of State, Defense, and Energy, and eliminate the responsibility of exporters to "know" the destinations and uses of their products. In addition, several industry groups are lobbying to have all computers removed from all control lists because they assert that computers are not required to make first generation nuclear bombs.[26] This assertion ignores overwhelming evidence that computers can and do assist a wide spectrum of weapons development activities.[27]

The policy attempts to compensate for the deregulation of sensitive technology by singling out a few "rogue nations" for exclusion from the new world of "increasingly open trade and technology for those states that live by accepted international rules."[28] In the past, however, even allies have disagreed about which countries are "rogues" and which are legitimate customers. Iran provides a good example of the difficulties with this approach: U.S. diplomats have had little success in dissuading Europe, Russia, China, and even U.S. companies from doing a robust trade with Tehran.[29] A nonproliferation policy based on identifying "rogue nations" is bound to fail.[30]

Choosing between unfettered trade and effective nonproliferation has never been easy. In the past the United States has been more will-

---

[24] Trade Promotion Coordinating Committee, Report to Congress, *Toward a National Export Strategy*, September 30, 1993, p. 57.

[25] The new policy would most affect items on the Department of Commerce Commodity Control List such as computers, telecommunications technology, advanced electronics, and machine tools.

[26] Petition of the American Electronics Association, pursuant to section 789.3 of the Export Administration Regulations, before the United States Department of Commerce, Bureau of Export Administration; "US Acts to Ease Export Controls on Computers," *Washington Post*, August 27, 1993, B1.

[27] See a joint report by three U.S. nuclear weapons laboratories, "The Need for Supercomputers in Nuclear Weapons Design," U.S. Department of Energy, January 1986.

[28] President Clinton, speech before the United Nations, September 27, 1993.

[29] "Clinton to Press Yeltsin on Arms to Iran," Reuters, January 8, 1994; "Technology From West Floods Iran," *Washington Post*, November 10, 1992; "German Exports Helping Iran Rebuild, Rearm," *Washington Post*, December 6, 1992; "Outlaw Iran Given World Bank Loan" *Washington Post*, March 31, 1993; "Suppliers of Dual Use Technology to Iran," compiled by the Subcommittee on International Security, International Organizations and Human Rights, Committee on Foreign Affairs, October 26, 1993.

[30] See Senator John Glenn, "Revenge of the Rogues," *Proliferation Watch*, March-April 1993.

ing than other nations to forego profits for security. This may be changing. Efforts to reinvigorate the U.S. economy appear to have shifted the balance away from nonproliferation towards policies to boost exports and create jobs. With this shift could come an increase in the probability that U.S. and allied troops will once again face weapons of mass destruction that have "Made in America" printed on them. The same holds true for all members of the Western alliance.

One possible rejoinder to this argument is the new emphasis on counterproliferation. Although there is still confusion about the meaning of the term, counterproliferation presumably refers to military responses to proliferation. The Clinton administration created a new assistant secretary of defense for nuclear security and counterproliferation, but the relationship between traditional nonproliferation and counterproliferation (and the bureaucracies that are responsible for them) has yet to be clarified. Nevertheless, a new emphasis on military responses might be viewed as a counterbalance to an increasing proliferation threat.

Critics of this approach assert that it is far less costly in the long run to prevent proliferators from acquiring destabilizing weapons in the first place than to wage war to eliminate those weapons after they are deployed. Most of the short term economic benefits derived from a liberalized export policy would probably be negated by the human, political, and material costs of war. Moreover, counterproliferation may not work. A recent Pentagon analysis calls into question previous claims about the effectiveness of air strikes against known nuclear sites in Iraq during the Gulf war. Military officials have also cast doubt on the future prospects for bombing nuclear facilities, even if the United States is sometimes prepared to take unilateral action. The standoff with North Korea has focused attention on the limitations of counterproliferation policy.[31]

AN ALTERNATIVE APPROACH

Rather than loosening controls and preparing to counter proliferation with force, a better strategy would be to strengthen the nonproliferation regime. It is possible to improve the effectiveness of export controls without sacrificing business interests. Beyond simply expanding membership and control lists, there are many ways to strengthen the regimes.

Implementation and enforcement of existing multilateral controls could be upgraded and standardized. Information on licensing decisions,

---

[31] Tony Capaccio, "New Report: Air Strikes Against Iraq's Key Nuke Site Were Wanting," *Defense Week*, January 10, 1994, p.1.

including denials, could be shared through the use of computer data bases. To further the emerging norm of transparency, IAEA has proposed a registry for all nuclear commerce -- an idea that incorporates concepts from the United Nations arms transfer registry.[32] In a similar vein, intelligence sharing has made great strides as a result of international efforts to stop Iraq's and North Korea's clandestine weapons programs. Informal agreements such as the NSG and the MTCR could be formalized through treaties that include verification and enforcement mechanisms. Some have suggested designating proliferation as an international crime, for which accused individuals could be extradited.[33] Another possibility would be to consolidate the regimes to better coordinate joint actions.[34] Finally, Senator John Glenn introduced legislation that would strengthen the U.S. and international agencies that are responsible for implementing (and enforcing) nonproliferation.[35]

Of course, all of these efforts to improve export controls are most effective when they are part of a comprehensive nonproliferation strategy. Such a strategy should aim to preserve the NPT, strengthen the IAEA and its safeguards system, promote U.N.-sponsored enforcement of the NPT, and reduce reliance on nuclear weapons through arms control.[36] A comprehensive strategy would build on existing nonproliferation norms and institutions to prevent the devolution of the regime.

SECURITY, ECONOMICS, AND THE AMERICAN MISSION AFTER THE COLD WAR

Ideology may play a role in shaping the new American policy. Some who advocate deregulating sensitive dual-use technology are motivated by parochial interests, but in a broader sense there is

---

[32] On the emerging norm of transparency see Edward Laurance, "Transparency in Armaments," *Missile Monitor*, Monterey Institute of International Studies, Spring 1992, p.4.

[33] Many of these ideas are outlined in Burrus Carnahan and Eve Cohen, *Enhancing the Effectiveness of Nonproliferation Export Controls*, Science Applications International Corporation, Report for the Department of Energy, March 1993.

[34] For analysis of the prospects of regime consolidation see Leonard Spector and Virginia Foran, *Preventing Weapons Proliferation: Should the Regimes Be Combined?* Report of the Thirty-Third Strategy for Peace, US Foreign Policy Conference, October 1992; and Gary Bertsch and Richard Cupitt "Nonproliferation and Export Controls," *Washington Quarterly*, Autumn 1993.

[35] S. 1055, Nuclear Export Reorganization Act of 1993, *Congressional Record*, May 27, 1993, S6772.

[36] On a comprehensive strategy see *Strengthening the Non-Proliferation Regime: 1995 and Beyond*, Oxford Research Group, Report Number 13, December 1993; and a special issue of the journal *Disarmament* on Strengthening the NPT and the Nuclear Non-Proliferation Regime, United Nations, Volume XVI, Number 2, 1993.

widespread consensus on the benefits of free trade. The bipartisan nature of the consensus was evident in the debate over the North American Free Trade Agreement and in our relations with China. This ideology of free trade is linked to the belief that free market economies are the surest route to democracy. Consequently, promoting economic freedom is viewed as essential for democratization in Eastern Europe, Russia, China, and elsewhere. Of course, spreading democracy is an historic mission of the United States. This mission may have renewed appeal after the death of communism. It is unfortunate that fundamental aspects of nonproliferation policy such as export controls are viewed as a hinderance to free trade and the democratization process.

It is true that economic interests have a new urgency in the post Cold War era. In many ways economics may surpass in importance the traditional military components of national power. Geopolitics are not dead, however. Loosening export controls probably won't fix the American economy or solve the economic problems of Europe. Moreover, if proliferation threats do not evaporate and the U.S. and Europe -- the core of the nonproliferation regime -- agree to preserve rather than weaken the regime, we may see a reassessment of the costs *and benefits* of nonproliferation export controls. Spreading economic prosperity and democracy depends on a stable foundation of peace and security.

CHAPTER 5

FINANCING THE ARMS TRADE[*]

Ian Anthony
Arms Production and Arms Transfer Project
SIPRI, Stockholm

INTRODUCTION

For reasons outlined below, it is likely than in the future the international arms market will operate in a manner that more closely resembles the market for major civil goods - through the dynamics of the tow markets will never be identical. In these circumstances the issue of financing arms transfers seems certain to become a more and more significant factor in determining the volume and pattern of the trade in major conventional weapons.

It would be difficult to exaggerate the role that the collapse of the former Soviet Union and the change in US - Soviet/Russian relations that resulted for it played in bringing about this change. Between the late 1940s and roughly 1990, the global arms trade was dominated by two superpowers that used arms transfers to support wider foreign and security policies in the framework of the Cold War For the superpowers economic benefits derived from foreign sales were secondary to their cold war competition. To advance their position vis-à-vis, one another both superpowers were prepared to subsidize their arms exports or, under certain conditions, give away equipment.

With the removal of the competitive ideological dimension from superpower relations the willingness of either the US or Russia to offer grant military assistance to arms clients has declined. IN policy statement by both of the major arms producers in the world the eco-

---

[*] Paper prepared for the Centre of Defence Studies Workshop on the European Arms Trade and the EC, 18-19 January 1994.

nomic and employment befits from foreign sales are now more heavily stressed than before.

The unit cost of major weapons is so great that relatively few countries are able to afford them if asked to pay with cash either in advance or with a single lump-sum. As a result, financial aspects of arms transfers are likely to have a more central bearing on success of failure in the marketplace. This change was already underway before the end of the cold war, especially for the group of countries which faced the problem of servicing a mounting burden of foreign debt. One US executive who had experience with both United Technologies and Westinghouse before the end of the cold war has said (only half in fun) that potential customers for major weapons really wanted to discuss performance characteristics or delivery dates before the issues of financing and the value of offsets have been explored in negotiations.[1] This observation is supported by the discussion in the United Kingdom of the financing arms transfers to Malaysia and Saudi Arabia under government-to-government agreements concluded between 1985 and 1988.

In the 1950s, both superpowers tended to offer arms on a grant of soft credit basis. Through the 1960s, a more commercial approach to arms transfers gained ground progressively until the late 1970s. However, according to Michael Brzoska, 'It is most probable the complex financing of arms deals increased in importance throughout the 1980s and even more so in the 1990s.[2] In the immediate aftermath of the end of the cold war the disposal of surplus equipment associated with the demilitarization of Germany has to some extent, dampened this tendency towards the sale of new equipment. However, this has been a temporary phenomenon which is almost complete.

For arms recipients credit-worthiness and the extent to which the international community decides to tie economic assistance to evaluations of arms procurement decisions will go some way to defining whether they are able to purchase major system. At the same time, the primary purpose of arms procurement is to contribute to the military capability of the armed forces. The level of armed forces maintained and their capability are ultimately tied to perception about external threat. In the face of a significant external threat, real or perceived, there are many historical examples of states prepared to allocate a major share of human and material resources to defence regardless of the distorting effect this may have on the economy.

---

[1] Ellen Frost speaking at the workshop on Conventional Arms Proliferation in the 1990,s, Carnegie Endowment for International Peace, 9-10 July 1992. Frost in now Counselor to the US Trade Representative Mickey Knator.

[2] Broska, M., 'The Financing Factor in Military Trade,' Defence and Peace Economics, vol. 5 no. 1 1994, pp. 67-80.

Apart form the United States and Russia, the third major centre for arms production in the world is Europe.[3] As pointed out in the introduction, in the absence of a common foreign and security policy a single European arms export policy cannot be developed by governments. Moreover, in the absence of a common defence policy the growth emergence of an integrated European defence industry is unlikely.

In spite of the changed political conditions it is likely that prospective recipients take into account politics of security assistance in evaluating suppliers. The correlation between arms transfers and major alliances is close, given the importance attached to equipment standardization as an element of operational efficiency. Purchasing a major system also brings close contact with the armed forces of the supplier state for training and logistical support. Even in the absence of any security guarantee, a close arms transfer relationship may suggest that the supplier government has a stake in the security of the recipient. The emergence of a common foreign and security policy would be likely to make European suppliers more interesting in the eyes of recipients seeking political dividends form from an arms transfer relationship. The development of a common defence policy could offer European companies research and development resources and a scale of production that would enhance their competitiveness.

In the absence of these benefits a European exporter who cannot put together a 'package deal' that includes financing as some form of offset is at a competitive disadvantage even if the equipment offered is of proven quality and of the current generation.

As this brief discussion suggest, arms procurement is still different in important respects form other forms of government expenditure and international trade. From the supply side, at the national level governments will continue to insist on maintaining close oversight and political control over decisions to export military equipment. Meanwhile the demand for conventional weapons is likely to be driven primarily by judgments reached by governments about their security environment.

Nevertheless, the differences between major arms procurement programmes and major capital projects in the civil sector may be diminishing. If so, then the issue of financing arms transfers is likely to be on the agenda of the European Union (EU) given its role in making and implementing foreign trade policy. EU interest may be even stronger in cases where arms transfers between member states and non-members are one element in a trade package that includes civil items that fall under existing EU competence.

Recent public disclosures related to several events have attracted attention to possible negative consequences of the lack of regulation

---

[3] Although Russia is a European country, for the purposes of this discussion it is useful to treat it as a separate entity.

within the international financial sector in respect of military-related projects. Arrangements established between the Italian Banca Nazionale del Lavoro (BNL) and Iraq in the context of legitimate arms transfers were used by Iraq to finance the procurement of equipment and materials for its chemical and nuclear weapons programmes. Meanwhile, the Bank of Credit and Commerce International (BCCI) held private accounts holding monies generated by government-sponsored arms transfers (among other transactions) that were never declared to national authorities. The issues raised by these aspects of arms transfer financing are different from those discussed elsewhere in the paper. First, these transactions involve criminal behavior; second, they can only be addressed through multinational measures and third, they are peripheral to the arms trade - which is overwhelmingly a government-managed activity. For these reasons the issuer of bank regulation is not returned to below.

Rahter, the paper will survey some of the existing arrangements and instruments used to finance arms transfers in the United States], the former Soviet Union and Europe. The paper concludes with a discussion of how this emerging issue might be addressed in the context of the European Union.

EXPORT CREDIT AND OFFSETS

The issues involved in financing arms transfers can be divided into tow groups: those which monetary instruments directly and those which use non-monetary forms of compensation. These financing tools are not mutually exclusive and could all be used in the package of arrangements associated with the same bi-lateral transfer. Moreover, the definitions offered here are no definitive and can probably be refined further as part of the development of theory in this area. For example, it would be hard to classify a commercial transaction that involved capital investment in civil production in the buyer country; the establishment of a local subsidiary or industrial joint venture.

The first group of issues can be sub-divided into export credit and aid. Export credit allows a recipient to defer payment for any goods or services purchased. This may be through a bi-lateral agreement that payments will begin after a certain period has elapsed or through the arrangement of a loan. Loans may involve the use of public funds of various kinds or private sector funds. Aid allows a value to be placed on a given transfer but does not involve any payment. The second group of issues can be labeled offsets. As defined by Stepanie Neuman in 1985, offsets are 'agreements that incorporate some method of reducing the amount of foreign exchange needed to buy a military item of some

means of creating revenue to pay for it.[4] Co-production, countertrade and barter are forms of offset.

In all cases of major equipment sales, government and industry work closely together. This cooperation is central to success in exporting. However, the nature of financial support offered to exporters by the major suppliers is different. Among the major exporter, the United States has by far, the largest and most thoroughly developed system for financing arms exports. Only Russia and China of the moor arms producing countries, could aspire to a comparable system under present conditions. For smaller European countries, the development of a more substantive arms export financing system would depend on the development off an integrated European military establishment, something which is not an immediate prospect.

EXPORT CREDIT

In international trade in civil goods, some countries have come together to agree rules for export financing. The most important of these groupings is the Organization for Economic Cooperation and Development (OECD) which adopted the Arrangement on Guidelines for Officially Supported Export Credits in March 1988. As a supplement of the general arrangement, four special sector agreements were signed to cover ships, nuclear power plants, large non-nuclear power generating plants and aircraft.[5] However, in the agreement, military goods (as well as agricultural commodities) are explicitly excluded form the terms and conditions. Consequently, OECD countries are free to establish the parameters for arms expert financing on a national basis.

Whether this continues to be true, is open to doubt. As the need to cooperate against a Soviet military threat has faded, allies in North America, Europe and Asia are paying proportionately greater attention to industrial competitiveness and major arms contracts are unlikely to be excluded from this competition.

To take one (perhaps the clearest) example, West European armies manufactures have invested considerable energy in developing markets in southeast Asia. However, the more valuable east Asian markets of Japan, South Korea and Taiwan are dominated by US suppliers. It is predictable that as the US military presence in Asian diminishes on the one hand, and the self-confidence and self-reliance of Asian countries grows on the other, European companies will seek to expand their

---

[4]Coproduction, Barter, and Countertrade: Offsets in the International Arms Market,' Orbis, vol. 29 no. 1, Spring 1985, p. 183.

[5]These agreements are reproduced as appendices in the The Export Credit Financing Systems in OECD Member Countries, (OECD: Paris 1990).

presence in these countries. If such competition was to be unregulated, then disputes about the fairness of trading practices are inevitable. In a political climate where preventing disputes over economic issues from disrupting long establish political relationships, there are likely to be pressures for a 'level playing field' for arms transfers. Within NATO, the discussion a defence trade 'code of conduct' has been underway for several years and a draft document has been near to completion for some time. In December 1993, NATO officials revealed that they had the consent of all parties around a draft document. However, it was not possible to finesse the remaining disagreements between the United States and Turkey. The basis for the code of conduct is transparency and advance notification of future equipment requirements and non-discrimination in contract awards. However, even if such a code can be implemented within NATO (something which has yet to be demonstrated) it would be difficult to expand such practices to cover trade with countries beyond the alliance.

UNITES STATES EXPORT FINANCING

In the United States, the government has several means of financing arms transfers. These consist of the Foreign Military Financing programme (FMF), a Military Assistance Programme (MAP) and the Excess Defense Articles (EDA) programme. In addition, overseas customers also benefit indirectly r he manner in which the US Department of Defense (specifically the Defense Security Assistance Agency (DSAA)) manages the Foreign Military Sales (FMS) programme. Other programmes - the Economic Support Fund (ESF) and International Military Education and Training (IMET) are indirectly relevant but peripheral to the question of financing arms transfers and these are not considered further in this essay.

Of these programmes, the most important in terms of the value of direct assistance offered is the Foreign Military Finance programme. The latest figures available for the DSAA are currently preliminary and not final. However, they indicate that for fiscal year 1994, the total value of FMF credit extended to foreign governments for the procurement of defense articles or services will be $3.1 billion. The value of FMF credit has been declining since 1983, when it reached a peak of almost $6 billion.

The FMF programme has been restructured after 1985 in a series of changes to the Arms Export Control Act. The original intention of FMF was to act as a transition for countries moving off military assistance programmes. Gradually, assistance was to be replaced with low-interest loans, which could be used to purchase US equipment, either under the FMS programme or on a commercial basis. However, the proportion of grant aid to loans has progressively grown in recent years.

FMF credit is tow kinds: loans and grants. Loans are mad by the Federal Financing Bank (administered by the US Department of the Treasury). Originally intended to be at the same commercial rate which the S government could obtain in the private sector. However, during the late 1908's as interest rates grew, 'concessional loans' - loans at interest rates below the commercial market rate - were offered to recipients in difficulty over repayment. FMF grants are technically known as 'forgiven loans' but as repayment is waived these are, in effect, grant assistance.

In recent years, the balance between the two forms of credit has been uneven, with the great majority of FMF credit being in the form of forgiven loans. Israel and Egypt are the primary beneficiaries of foreign loans, together accounting for abut 75 percent of the entire FMF programme.

The Military Assistance Programe has greatly decline d in importance in comparison with the period from around 1950 through the 1970s. Military assistance is programmed on a country-by-county basis to pay for military material and services provided by the United States at no cost to the recipient. In recent years, the value of MAP has never exceeded $180 million. Most of this being allocated to Turkey (including funds for the operation to provide relief to Kurdish refugees in Iraq) and Latin American countries participating in the US Andean initiative to reduce the volume of illegal drug trade.

Overseas recipients of US excess defence articles - items procured for but no longer needed by the US armed forces - my have benefited from the manner in which DOD pricing directives have been interpreted. Under DOD pricing directives, used equipment should be valued at a percentage of its original acquisition value up to a ceiling of 50 percent. However, these directives are only guidelines and are not followed in all cases.

An indirect form of export financing is provided by the manner in which FMS negotiations are conducted. Contracts are made between US private sector arms producers and the DOD which negotiates separate agreements with foreign governments. In negotiation on price with a manufacturer, the DOD combines foreign orders with order for the US armed forces in order to achieve economies of scale and drive down the unit cost of equipment.

In 1991 and 1992, considerable controversy was raised by a proposal that the Export-Import Bank (a branch of the US Agency for International Development within the State Department) would have a $1 billion fund established specifically for use in providing loan guarantees for commercial arms transfer transactions. In 1993, the issue was raised again in the context of President Clinton' plan to provide up o $20 billion worth of assistance to the US arms industry to manage the transition to lower levels of defence spending. Several US Senators have proposed using a proportion of this money (possibly up to $5 billion) to improve the international competitiveness of the US arms industry as a means of retaining production capacities.[6]

WEST EUROPEAN COUNTRIES

In all of the larger West European arms exporting countries the government offers some form of export financing assistance to industry. This is usually indirect assistance offered by specialized agencies. One form of assistance, offered by bodies such as the UK Defence Export Services Organisation or the French SOFMA (Societe Francaise de Materiels d'Armement), is market analysis that helps identify potential sales opportunities and assists the marketing efforts of companies. Another form of assistance is offered by some government export finance agencies - such as the Export Credit Guarantee Department in the UK, the COFACE (Compagnie Francaise d'Assurance du Commerce Exterieur) in France and Hermes credit guarantee programe in Germany - which extended insurance coverage for defence contracts.

In a classified memo from the German Ministry of Finance to the Bundestage, it was revealed that 10 of the 17 credit guarantee programmes managed by the Hermes are military programmes with coverage worth DM 2.26 billion.[7]

This provision of insurance for transfers to developing countries became more important to suppliers in the 1980's as commercial financial institutions were heavily exposed to possible defaults as a result of loans already made to developing countries. In spite of several studies no clear link has been established between arms imports and heavy indebtedness.[8] Nevertheless, it is certainly true that some of the countries with a relatively high burden of external debt-service are or have been significant arms importers. This is true for some countries of Latin America (such as Argentina), the Middle East (such s Jordan and Egypt) and Asia (such as Pakistan). The most spectacular example of a default clearly attributable to arms imports is that of Iraq, which had accumulated almost $10 billion worth of debts, mainly to France and the former Soviet Union, at the time its assets were frozen in the context of UN sanctions.

---

[6] The US debate on this issue is summarized in a newsletter produced by Lora Lumpe of the Federation of American Scientist, Arms Sales Monitor Alert! 20 May 1993

[7] Welwirtschaft & Entwicklung, 7 Jan. 1994.

[8] For example. Somnath Sen, 'Debt, Financial Flows and International Security,' SIPRI Yearbook 1990, (Oxford University Press, Oxford 1990).

EXPORT FINANCING IN THE TRANSITION ECONOMIES

In spite of the declining volume of sales in recent years, the countries of Central and Eastern Europe (defined to include Russian and the other independent states established on the territory of the former Ukrania Union) still retain significant industrial capacities. Russia is still an important arms exporter and recent data suggest that the Ukrainian defence industry has also been successful in winning some exports. Elsewhere I Central and Eastern Europe, it is unlikely that defence industries have any long term prospects of survival, except for one or two companies operating in certain niche markets.

Among the members of the Warsaw Treaty Organization (WTO) financial and trade systems were closely integrated in a centralized planning system. In general arms transfers were considered as an element of foreign and defence policy and as such, treated as a political rather than a trade issue. A significant proportion of total Soviet arms transfers to developing countries took the form of grant assistance with the recipient paying nothing for the equipment received. This form of transfer has been terminated entirely.

Government-to-government negotiations were central to the administration of exports. As a result, the sudden winding up of the Council for Mutual Economic Assistance (CMEA) contributed to the rapid decline in trade which has produced and economic crisis for industrial production of al kinds in Central and Eastern Europe.[9]

Within the WTO interstate financial transfers associated with arms transfers and defence industrial cooperation were agreed on the basis of convertible roubles using an exchange rate fixed by negotiation between the various central planning agencies rather than through the operation of the market. In turn, the financial flows form government to the producers themselves were determined by central government on the basis of an artificial exchange rate.[10] Similarly, in both transfers between the government and industry goods were priced through an administrative decision rather than to reflect the costs of inputs and the need for profit.

Somewhat similar bureaucratic arrangements were made between the former Soviet Union and major arms recipients. The primary beneficiaries of credit arrangements were Algeria, Iraq, Libya, Syria and India - which was able to make purchase both in exchange for commodities (The Soviet Union maintained a rupee account used to pur-

---

[9]The issue of financing is taken up in Anthony, I. (ed) The Future of Defence Industries in Central and Eastern Europe, SIPRI Research Report no. 7, (Oxford University Press: Oxford 1994).

[10]A useful summary of CMEA trade relations is 'The Collapse of Trade Among Former Members of the CMEA,' a survey prepared by staff of the IMF contained in World Economic Outlook, Washington DC Oct. 1991.

chase goods in India) and against a credit account establish at the Indian central bank. Credit was repayable over up to 17 years with an interest rate of around 2 percent. However, since neither the rupee nor the rouble is a convertible currency , the true balance of Indo-Soviet trade is also almost impossible to establish.[11]

In December 1990, the Soviet Union prohibited barter trade with former CMEA partners. With the termination of the CMEA relationship in 1991, all of the countries of Central and Eastern Europe initially decided to conduct foreign trade on the basis of hard currency payment. By mid 1991, the Soviet Union had lifted the prohibition on barter and by 1994, almost all Central and East European countries have retreated form their decision to trade only in hard currency having found it almost impossible to conclude sales on the basis.

By 1993, elements of the WTO defence industrial cooperation and arms trade relationships had been reestablished without accompanying hard currency payments. In most cases, these were bilateral links with Russia, the primary source of technology and products, as well as the primary market for military equipment in the region. Similarly, not only India but other important customers (notably China and Iran) arranged transfers on the basis of part-payment in commodities.

The decisions by Hungary and Slovakia in 1993 to accept MiG-29 fighter aircraft and other military equipment from Russia as partial settlement of Russian debt also reflects an interesting new development in financing. The process through which the level of bilateral debt was establish and for establishing the value of goods transferred both appear to have been somewhat arbitrary.[12]

The government of Russia has taken steps to establish agencies to assist industry in winning arms exports. In addition, recent public statement shy official, most notably Vice Premier Alexander Shokhin, have suggested that export financing of some kinds will be available in future an aid to industry.[13] Among the indirect forms of assistance presently offered are marketing surveys and subsidies to cover the cost of attending overseas defence exhibitions. Russian banks are being actively drawn into the process of restructuring the defence industry and

---

[11]This became a major issue between India and Russia during the visit to New Delhi of President Yeltsin in January 1993. Russians, arguing that the oil, natural gas and capital goods transferred to India had been heavily undervalued, claimed a major debt was owed to them by India. Indi, meanwhile, pointed to the fact that in bilateral trade agreements the rouble was significantly overvalued. In the end, the compromise reached includes large elements taken directly from past arrangements including significant barter and long-term credit.

[12]Although in both cases the aircraft transferred were produced in the past tow years - that is, after the beginning f the Gaidar economic reform programme - administrative price controls have not been lifted for the defence sector.

[13]Shokhin is head of the Interdepartmental Commission on Military Technical Cooperation with Foreign Countries.

credit facilities are likely to be available to any arms producer which
can find customers able to make payments in hard currency or material
that can relatively easily be turned into hard currency.

OFFSETS

In the absence of a US-style system for financing exports, West European producers have developed alternative strategies in an effort to
remain competitive. Offset packages, sometimes negotiated under the
umbrella of government-to-government memoranda of understanding,
have been the most effective of these strategies.

The term offset is used to cover a wide range of different non-monetary transactions linked to transfers of defence equipment of services.
Offsets are said to be direct if they are linked directly to the military
goods or services which are being bought and indirect if they relate to
some other goods or series. Industrial transactions might include coproduction of the equipment to be bought; licensed production of the
equipment to be bout; production of some part of component of the
equipment or a technology transfer of some kind. countertrade can also
be of various kinds, including counter-purchase (agreement by the seller
to purchase goods or services for the buyer to an agreed value) or buy-
back (in which the seller agrees to purchase goods or series that the
buyer generates thorough an industrial offset). Recent examples of
barter include the possibility that Russia will accept palm oil for
Malaysia in exchange for MiG-29 fighter aircraft and the possibility
that Ukraine will provide Iran with military goods and services in exchange or oil.

These arrangements are widely regarded by industrial representatives as a 'necessary evil' at best, and are often criticized as undesir-
able distortions of free trade.[14] In the United States, Alan Shaw of the
Office for Technology Assessment has put forward other arguments
against industrial offsets, namely that they make the US 'dependent
on potentially unreliable foreign sources, erode the UF defence industrial base, take business away form US companies and jobs away form
American workers and transfer to competitors, valuable technology
that will come back to haunt our civilian markets.'

This debate does no have quite the same resonance in Europe where
national budgets are clearly unable to support a wide-ranging defence
industry offsets are Hobson's Choice.

The impact of offsets is impossible to examine because there is an
almost complete lack of data. In response to a 1985 amendment to the

---

[14]Joel Johnon of the US Aerospace Industries Association has observed that if arrangements
of this kind were preferable, it would not have been necessary to invent money.

Defense Production Act, the US Office of Management and Budget (OMB) established a database to record offsets on military sales for the period beginning fiscal year 1980, Reports on offsets are submitted annually, including assessment of the impact of offsets on industrial competitiveness and employment. According to this information, which is derived form a detailed questionnaire sent to US defence contractors by the OMB, during the 1980's. the value of offset agreements amounted to 57 percent of the value of arms export agreements.[15] No other country prepares aggregate assessments of this type for public release. The absence of comprehensive data measures contributes to the politicization of the debate over the impact of offsets.

The decision to establish a turnkey production line in Saudi Arabia to produce printed electronic circuit boards could be cited as an example of the difficulty of using anecdotal evidence to resolve analytical problems. This production line has as its primary customer General Dynamics, maker of the M-1 Abrams tank whose purchase led to its establishment.[16] In the absence of the Sause facility, General Dynamics might buy components from a US supplier (or it might not). In any event, GD buys form the Advanced Electronics Center not from choice but because it is obliged to do so, and when this formal commitment ends, it may find al alternative supplier. This will leave the Saudi facility - which represents a considerable financial and human investment - with an uncertain future as there is little domestic demand for its products.

Others argue that with or without arms transfer related offsets, the US defence industry is likely to become more dependent on foreign suppliers. Similarly, increased technology transfers and transnational industrial linkages are likely to be adopted unilaterally by industry as responses to the changed market conditions they are confronting. Meanwhile, US market share seems to be growing rapidly, at least for those parts of the defence sector which we think we can measure. Therefore, the argument runs, formal offset arrangements do little more than codify transactions which would occur anyway and so, have little effect, either positive or negative, on trade flows.

The offset arrangements associated with the purchase of E-3 Sentry AWACS form the United States by the United Kingdom and France in 1986 and 1987 respectively, might be cited in the is context. These arrangements were heavily criticized in the United States at the time they were singed because they involved offsets worth more than the

---

[15] Offsets in Military Exports, Executive Office of the President of the United States, Dec. 1988.

[16] The Advanced Electronics Center (AEC) handles several other offset arrangements involving the production of components thorough joint ventures with Boeing (USA) and Racal (UK).

value of the contract secured. In the case of the UK, the offset package was worth 130 percent of the value of the aircraft. A few years later, however, the critics of the arrangement were primarily to be found in the UK - where it was argued that there was little evidence of new investment in Britain or overseas contracts for British companies arising out of the offset package. GEC, which was the main UK contractor involved in the programme, has increased its sales in the United States. however, this has been at the centre of the company's business strategy and my well have occurred without any formal offset arrangements.

It is difficult to measure the impact of transactions which span several years and in some cases, more than a decade. A final calculation about whether or not obligations were satisfied, can't be made until the end of the arrangement and perhaps not for several years after that. At this point, the agreed party is like to find it difficult to get redress.

Offsets are likely to add complexity to overall bilateral national trade relations. Government involvement is almost always required to establish an umbrella memorandum of understanding. Moreover, n cases where one or other party is dissatisfied with the implementation of agreements, government agencies are again, likely to involved in negotiations. In cases such as the 1985 and 1988 memoranda of understanding between the UK and Saudi Arabia, known as Al Yamamah I and Al Yamamah II, the government of Saudi Arabia agreed to set aside a specified volume of oil to pay for defence equipment and services purchase form several British companies (though British Aerospace is by far the largest supplier). As the price of oil has been progressively falling, however, it has proved necessary to renegotiate the agreement as British companies no longer felt that they were receiving a fair price.

Implementing offset agreements can also involve companies in complex new business activities where they have no specialist expertise. In managing the offsets associated with Al Yamamah British Aerospace was forced to seek arrangement with British Petroleum (to manage oil shipments), Leyland DAF, Rolls Royce, pharmaceuticals company Glaxo and sugar refiner Tate & Lyle. British Aerospace also bought a Dutch construction company to carry out offset-related work.

The agreement also commits British companies to invest I Saudi Arabia in projects designed to develop the local technology base. This aspect of the package has proved difficult to implement as the capacity of Saudi Arabia to abuser technology transfers is limited by the shortage of Saudi technicians able to be employed in new ventures.

As there is no aggregate measure of the impact of offsets, it is impossible to say with any certainty wheeler the use of offsets is increasing or decreasing. In some countries- for example, Greece, Soth Korea and Taiwan - offsets are mandatory and are written into government procurement regulations. Governments must achieve a minim offset requirement (expressed as a percentage of the contract value) before any contract can legally be awarded., Again however, there is no survey available which indicates how widespread this approach to procurement is or how the tend is developing.

CONCLUSIONS

This paper has been able to do no more than raise interesting questions about the relationship between the international arms trade and finance. That there is a relationship between trade and financing is obvious, However, the special nature of the arms trade introduces several complications. The arms trade has been explicitly exempted for the regulations which have been developed to govern the financing of civilian trade.[17] Governments are allowed to subsidize exports of arms to whatever level they choose directly or indirectly, without penalty. There in no evidence that governments intend to give up their capacity to intervene in defence industrial issues. Moreover, there is no international consensus about the definition of conventional arms. Therefore, the issue of arms export financing contains the seeds of political disputes if it is suspected that the definition of arms is being stretched to give any country an advantage in what other see as a civil transaction

Efforts to develop rules defining what are 'fair and unfair arms trade practices have been made within the NATO alliance. Although these intra-alliance discussions have not produced any tangible result, it seems likely that a broader approached will be attempted given the implication of the end of the cold war and the emergence of Russian arms producers into a more global arms market. The issue of export financing would be a logical issue to address in the framework of the GATT (especially within the new World Trade Organisation) and it seems likely to be only a matter of time before this occurs.

If this is so, it would be logical for the European Union - which is increasingly acknowledged as an important player in the GATT - as well as the individual member states to think through this issue.

Several questions need to be addressed.

- Should transfers of defense equipment be seen as a trade issue at all? Should such transfers be regarded rather as politico-military events (and therefore acts of foreign and

---

[17] It is perhaps worth noting at this point, that the regulations developed for civil sectors which have some characteristics in common with the arms industry - such as large commercial aircraft - have been notoriously difficult to enforce and allegations of violations are common.

security policy) with a limited economic dimension? If so, are arms transfers properly treated as an element in the common foreign and security policy?

- If arms transfers are seen as trade issues, then should they be integrated with the existing discussions of regulating global trade (many of which are conducted at the community level)? If so, what are the implications for national approaches to arms export policy?
- Is it possible to develop empirical measures of the incidence of 'managed trade' practices of various kinds? If so, are these practices increasing or decreasing?
- Where offsets occur what evidence is there that they meet the expectations of the recipient country? In defining their offset requirements, do recipients tend to take a technological approach (seeking access to specific technical capabilities for whatever reason) or a market approach (primarily evaluating the commercial prospects for offsets)?

CHAPTER 6

THE EUROPEAN UNION AND THE U.N. REGISTER OF CONVENTIONAL ARMS

Malcolm Chalmers and Owen Greene
Department of Peace Studies,
Bradford University

INTRODUCTION

The UN Register of Conventional Arms is a relatively rare example of a multilateral agreement relating to international security which EC states and Japan have jointly played a leading role in developing. It was these states that initially drafted a resolution for the UN First Committee in 1991 to set up a UN Register of International Conventional Arms Transfers, and subsequently reshaped and developed the proposal in order to achieve wide agreement to it. They played a key role in promoting wide participation in the first year of operation of the register, and will continue to have substantial influence over the ways in which this new UN transparency regime develops in the future. Moreover, as major arms producers, exporters and importers, EC states have a significant interest in the ways in which the Register develops and shapes debates about arms transfers and holdings.

The first report of the Register was released in October 1993, covering arms transfers for 1992[1]. In February 1994, a new UN Group of gov-

---

[1] *The United Nations Register of Convnetional Armaments; Report of the Secretary-General,* United Nations document A/48/344, 11 October 1993. For an analysis of the first report of the UN Register, see: M. Chalmers and O. Greene, *The United Nations Register of convnetional Armaments: an Initial Examination of the First Report,* Bradford Arms Register Studies (BARS)

ernmental experts convened to review the early experience with implementing the Register and to consider proposals for expanding and strengthening this new arms transparency regime. This panel is due to make recommendations for consideration by theUN First Committee in October 1994.

In the aftermath of the Gulf War and the end of the Cold War, the UN Register was one of the two main proposals for international actions to "do something" about the risks of destabilising build-ups of major conventional arms. The other proposal led to the P5 process, which arguably could have had a greater direct impact on the conventional arms trade than the UN Register. P5 discussions began in 1991, aimed at promoting arms export restraint amongst the P5 states, particularly in relation to transfers to the Middle East. During 1991 and 1992, these states - the five biggest suppliers of conventional arms - discussed proposals to harmonise their conventional arms export policies and to establish information-exchange and consultation arrangements. By promoting 'responsible' common guidelines and facilitating mutual consultations on potential major arms exports before final decisions had been taken, these arrangements could have significantly encouraged restraint amongst the major arms suppliers.

However, following the Bush Administration's decision in September 1992 to sell 150 US F-15 aircraft to Taiwan, the Chinese government withdrew from these discussions and the P5 process stalled. Since then, the UN Register of Conventional Arms has been the only significant multilateral agreement relating to conventional arms transfers (apart from specific arms embargoes directed against states such as former Yugoslavia, Iraq or Libya). In some ways, the UN Register is a modest development. Indeed this may be one of the reasons it has survived. It is a transparency measure, and does not involve controls on arms transfers. Participation is voluntary, and involves no acceptance of restrictions on arms transfers, production or holdings per se.

Nevertheless, the Register has potential value. It aims to improve transparency to build mutual confidence and facilitate timely interna-

No 2, Bradford University, October 1993; E. Laurance, S. Wezeman, and H. Wulf, *Arms Watch: SIPRI report on the first year of the UN Register of Conventional Arms*, SIPRI Research Report No 6, SIPRI/Oxford University Press, , 1993; BASIC, *Moving Toward Transparency: an evaluation of the United Nations Register of Conventional Arms*, BASIC Report 93.6, London/Washington DC, 1993. Other relevant articles and reports include: E. Laurence, 'The United Nations Register for Conventional Arms; rationales and prospects for compliance', *Washington Quarterly*, Vol 16, No 2, Spring 1993, pp 163 - 172; M. Chalmers and O. Greene, 'Implementing and Developing the United Nations Register of Conventional Arms', *Peace Research Reports Number 32*, University of Bradford, May 1993, pp120; H. Wagenmakers, 'The United Nations Register of Conventional Arms: a new instrument for collective security', *Arms Control Today* , Vol 23, No 3, April 1993, pp 16 - 21; I. Anthony, 'Assessing the UN Register of Conventional Arms', *Survival* , Vol 35, No 4, Winter 1993, pp 113 - 129;

tional consultations on potentially destabilising regional arms build-ups. Many hope that increased transparency (international and domestic) will also encourage restraint by exporting and importing states: it could increase the international and domestic pressures against "irresponsible" or potentially destabilising transfers. Moreover, there is real potential to develop the UN arms register transparency regime in the next few years - increasing transparency relating to arms transfers and expanding the Register to include national arms production and military holdings.

This chapter aims to discuss a number of aspects of the relationship between the UN Register and the European Union. The next section outlines the role that EU members played in the process of establishing the Register. This is followed by an examination of the information submitted by EU states (and by some prospective members) for the first annual report of the Register, and of some of the main issues raised by these submissions. The following section discusses the main issues on the agenda of the 1994 UN Group of Experts as they relate to EU states' interests and concerns. The chapter ends with some concluding remarks.

THE E.C. AND THE ESTABLISHMENT OF THE REGISTER

The origins of the UN Register of Conventional Arms can be traced back to the interwar period, when the League of Nations established transparency measures relating to international arms transfers. Between 1924 and 1938, it published an annual *Statistical Yearbook of the Trade in Arms, Munitions and Implements of War*[2]. Some 20 years after World War II, proposals to establish a transparency regime for arms transfers re-emerged, with proposals from Malta in 1965 and Denmark in 1967, followed by a similar initiative by Japan in 1976[3]. As international conditions became more favourable to such an initiative in the late 1980s, the UN General Assembly established an Expert Study Group to consider "ways and means of promoting transparency in international transfers of conventional arms on a universal and non-discriminatory basis"[4].

By the time this Expert Study Group reported in August 1991, the prospects for establishing such a Register had improved greatly. Soviet President Gorbachev's policy of glasnost and support for the UN ,

---

[2] J. Goldbalt, *Arms Control Agreements: a handbook*, Taylor & Francis, London 1982

[3] H. Wulf, 'United Nations deliberations on the arms trade', in I. Anthony (eds) *Arms Export Regulations*, Oxford University Press, 1991

[4] General Assembly Resolution 43/75 I, 'International Arms Transfers'.

combined with the demise of the Warsaw Treaty Organisation and the ending of the Cold War, removed a number of obstacles to the establishment of a Register. Moreover, in the immediate aftermath of the Gulf War in early 1991, there was strong pressure on governments to "do something" about the arms trade. On 8 February, 1991, the Canadian Prime Minister called for "early action on an information exchange system regarding arms transfers". Shortly afterwards, Canada issued its first Annual Report on Military Exports, detailing its arms exports for 1990. On 8 April, the British Prime Minister, John Major, called for a UN register of conventional arms transfers in a speech at the European Council in Luxembourg[5]. Several other EC states already had a record of supporting such proposals at the UN, and agreement amongst EC states to support such a proposal was rapidly achieved. They drafted a statement to the UN urging that the possibility of establishing a UN register be kept under review.

The proposal rapidly gained wide support. In May, Australia and the USSR endorsed the principle of a UN register of conventional arms transfers, and the USA had called for a meeting of the P5 to discuss the conventional arms trade. At the CSCE meeting on 19-20 June, all CSCE states reaffirmed the need for "restraint and transparency in the transfer of conventional weapons and weapons technologies, particularly to regions of tension"[6]. On 8-9 July, the P5 states agreed to support the establishment of a UN arms transfer register, to exercise restraint in arms transfers (particularly in the Middle East), and to develop mechanisms for mutual consultations and information exchange on arms transfers[7]. A few days later, the G7 meeting declared "we support the proposal for a universal register of arms transfers under the auspices of the United Nations and will work for its early adoption"[8].

In this context, the work of the UN Expert Study Group was encouraged and speeded up. It submitted its report to the UN Secretary General in September 1991. The report recommended that "a United Nations system should be established without delay to collect, process, and publish official standardised information on international arms transfers on a regular basis as supplied to the United Nations by member states on their arms exports and imports"..."Such a register should

---

[5] "Conventional Arms Transfers: background brief", Foreign and Commonwealth Office, UK, April 1992.

[6] "Summary of Conclusions", Berlin Meeting of the CSCE Council, 19-20 June, 1991.

[7] "Statement of the Permanent Five on Arms Transfers and Non-Proliferation", Paris, 8-9 July, 1991.

[8] "Declaration on Conventional Arms Transfers and NBC Non-Proliferation", Group of Seven Economic Summit, London 16 July, 1991.

be on a universal and non-discriminatory basis, including suppliers and recipients"[9].

The strong political support that had developed amongst powerful states for such a proposal during the preceding six months ensured that the Expert Study Group's report would be welcomed and rapidly followed up. However, the US administration was sceptical of the potential value of a UN Register, and decided to give higher priority to the development of the P5 process. This meant that active follow-up by western states of the recommendations of the Expert Study Group would be carried out, if at all, by US allies rather than the USA itself. The West European states, Japan and Canada were happy to play a prominent role in taking the issue forward.

In October, the 12 EC states and Japan circulated a draft resolution for the UN First Committee entitled "Transparency in Armaments", requesting the establishment of a "universal and non-discriminatory Register of International Conventional Arms Transfers"[10]. The draft resolution proposed a two-track approach: an arms transfer register would be established immediately, while the issue of reporting on military holdings and production would be referred to the Conference on Disarmament in Geneva. However, it soon became clear that this approach would have to be revised if the resolution was to achieve wide and early support amongst UN members. A number of developing, arms importing states, supported by Canada, criticised the resolution for excluding domestic procurement and holdings from the Register. Colombia and Peru supported a rival resolution directed mainly at limiting the illicit arms trade and which stopped short of proposing a UN Register. Several governments, such as India and China, were arguing for further study of the concept. In this context, the EC states and Japan revised their resolution with the aim of circumventing such obstacles and achieving wide agreement.

The revised resolution, endorsed also by Canada, the USSR, and several East European and Latin American states, was presented to the UN First Committee on 13 November. It called for the establishment of a UN Register of Conventional Arms (rather than simply arms transfers). Introducing this to the First Committee on the following day, the Dutch representative Mr Wagenmakers (speaking on behalf of the EC states while the Netherlands held the EC Presidency) said that it had been evident "that the scope of the [original] draft resolution had to be enlarged ...We recognised that this question had multiple facets:

---

[9] UN Experts Group Report to the Secretary-General, *Study on the ways and means of promoting transparency in international transfers of conventional arms*, UN Document A/46/301, 9 September 1991, paragraphs 25 and 26.

[10] Later to form the basis of UN First Committee, Draft Resolution A/C.1/46/L.18, presented on 31 October 1991.

transfers, production and stocks, and that these aspects are interrelated".[11] On the 15 November, the revised resolution was adopted by the First Committee by a vote of 106 in favour, one against (Cuba), and eight abstentions (China, North Korea, Iraq, Myanmar, Oman, Pakistan, Singapore, and Sudan). On 9 December, the UN General Assembly passed the resolution by 150 votes in favour with two abstentions (Cuba and Iraq).

Member states were requested to submit their first annual report (for 1992) by 30 April 1993. In the meantime, a panel of government experts was established to elaborate the Register's technical procedures and to prepare a report on what should be included in the Register, for submission in time for the First Committee to consider it in the autumn of 1992. This Panel of Experts consisted of 17 governmental experts. Each of the P5 states were represented, together with representatives from Ghana, Japan, Egypt, Brazil, Argentina, Mexico, Switzerland, Malaysia, Canada, India, the Netherlands, and the Czech and Slovak Federal Republic. It was chaired by the Dutch representative Mr Wagenmakers.

Thus EC states were well represented in the Panel. This was important since the Panel was a key negotiating forum for the establishment and early development of the Register. Moreover, the European experience with CSBMs and the CFE treaty shaped the way in which the Panel developed proposals for the categories of arms to be included in the Register. The EC states and the USA started by advocating that the Register should simply adopt CFE definitions of which types of tanks, aircraft, helicopters, heavy artillery and armoured personnel carriers that should be covered. However, countries represented on the panel that were not parties to the CFE treaty strongly resisted having pre-negotiated definitions foist upon them, and amended them significantly.

Nevertheless, the process of arriving at agreed definitions of arms categories for the Register undoubtedly benefitted from the background work carried out during the CFE negotiations. Whereas agreement was relatively easily achieved on the above five categories of arms, discussions on the categories of warships and missiles (which were not included in the CFE) were much more difficult. Fierce dispute about the threshold displacement tonnage above which warships should be reported was prolonged and the final recommendation to include all ships with displacement of more than 750 tonnes, plus those equipped for launching missiles or torpedoes with a range of 25 km or more, was a subject of some controversy. The missiles and missile launchers cate-

---

[11] Mr Wagenmakers, Dutch Representative, First Committee Verbatim Record A/C.1/46/PV.26.

gory that was agreed was widely perceived as being even more unsatisfactory. [12]

The Panel of Experts determined to take decisions by consensus. This was primarily due to the importance according to achieving wide participation in the Register from the outset. It also had the effect of greatly promoting the authority of Panel recommendations in the General Assembly, ensuring that they would be accepted without much dissent. The Panel reported on 17 July 1992[13], after four meetings.

As hoped, the report of the 1992 Panel of Experts was endorsed without significant changes by the UN General Assembly on 15 December 1992. Attention then turned to the task of encouraging states to submit reports for the Register, and providing them with technical guidance on how to complete the standardised form for submissions. This was a key phase in the establishment of the Register, and one in which the UN Office of Disarmament Affairs (ODA) could only play a limited role. Virtually no UN resources had been allocated for such training. Moreover, such was the sensitivity of this issue for some states that the ODA was instructed that it should not even take measures to remind states to submit their returns by 30 April 1993, still less was it allowed to participate in any interpretation of the Register's requirements or, subsequently, of national reports.

In this context, the process of promoting the establishment of the register depended on voluntary actions by states. Several EC states, including the Netherlands, Germany, France, Italy and the UK, played an active role in encouraging participation and facilitating the provision of technical assistance. Together with states such as Japan, Canada and Brazil, they contributed to the four regional workshops that were held in the spring of 1993. These were held in Tokyo, Florence, Warsaw and Buenos Aires. These workshops were important, not only in informing and training national officials on the requirements for submitting national reports for the· Register but also as a confidence building exercises: hesitant states were more ready to join the Register when it became clear in the course of their regional meeting that their neighbours intended to do so too. In addition to supporting and contributing to these workshops, EC states engaged in much bilateral diplomacy to encourage wide participation. This latter activity developed into an organised lobbying campaign, in which EC states divided responsibility amongst themselves to lobby large numbers of countries around the world.

---

[12] No differentiation is to be made between missiles and missile launchers, leading to an anomalous 'apples and pears' counting problem. Moreover, all ground-to-air missiles are excluded. See M. Chalmers and O. Greene, *Peace Research Report No 32, op cit*, for a further discussion of these issues.

[13] Report of the panel of governmental technical experts on the United Nations Register of Conventional Arms, UN Document A/47/342, 17 July, 1992.

In summary, EC states played an important role in the process of establishing the UN Register, together with countries such as Japan and Canada. They promoted and shaped the UN resolutions; participated actively in the Panels of Experts; devoted significant resources to providing technical assistance to countries wishing to make a submission to the Register; and lobbied to encourage wide participation.

In comparison, the United States played a less active role than the EC in promoting the Register at this stage. Initially, the Bush Administration regarded the Register as much less important than the P5 process. More broadly, US governments have tended to be relatively sceptical of UN-based cooperative regimes which do not impose specific restrictions on activities, regarding supplier regimes as more likely to be effective. Once the P5 process stalled, the United States supported the register more actively, but in general still without great enthusiasm.

In some ways the fact that the USA (and, a fortiori, Russia) did not play a leading role in promoting and developing the Register may have made it easier to promote wide support for the new transparency regime. It may have helped to reduce suspicion amongst developing and ex-Soviet states that the Register was being foist upon them by a superpower. European states were in a relatively good position to promote the Register. The important contribution that transparency and CSBM regimes have made to European security helped to convince UN members of the potential value of an arms register. Their experience with CSBMs gave them relative confidence in initiating and participating in transparency measures. Moreover, as discussed above, they could apply lessons from CFE treaty negotiations. However, developing countries' attitudes towards the significance of the European experience for the design of the Register were ambiguous. Any suggestion that "European models" of transparency regimes, inspired by the CSCE confidence and security-building measures or the CFE treaty, were being transferred to the rest of the world tended to be resented by developing countries. At that time, proposals to establish a CSCM (Conference on Security Cooperation in the Mediterranean) and a similar arrangement for the Asia-Pacific based on the CSCE, were being actively promoted by some EC states and their allies. These were resented by some states in the regions concerned.. In this context, it was important that countries outside Europe also played an important role in promoting the Register.

SUBMISSIONS TO THE FIRST REPORT
OF THE REGISTER

Participation in the Register in its first year of operation was larger than many anticipated. 80 states submitted reports in time for inclusion in the Secretary-General's 1993 report (covering 1992), including nearly all of the major arms exporting countries and most of the major arms importers.[14] After the publication of the Secretary-General's 1993 report, a few additional states also made returns - including Sri Lanka, Lebanon, and the Ukraine. It has been estimated that over 90% of global transfers of the major conventional armaments covered by the Register categories were included in the Register for 1992.[15] In view of the uncertain scale of covert arms trading, the reliability of such estimates is hard to assess, but it nevertheless seems clear that the overwhelming majority of major conventional arms transfers were reported.

All 12 members of the EC submitted returns for 1992 to the Register (as did all prospective members of the EC: that is, the EFTA states, the Visegrad four, (and also Romania, Bulgaria and Slovenia). The other Associate members of the EC, Turkey, Malta and Cyprus, also submitted returns. However Albania, Estonia and Latvia did not do so. According to data in the Register, three of the top six exporters of major conventional arms in 1992 (in terms of numbers of exported major arms) were members of the EC: Germany, France, and the UK. The latter two states have long been amongst the group of top arms exporters. Germany rose to the top in 1992 particularly due to transfers of equipment of former GDR forces. Italy and the Netherlands also emerge as major arms exporters in 1992.

It is important to note, however, that the Register focusses attention on numbers of transferred systems in each category, without requiring information on the types or value of the weapon systems involved. Clearly, for example, an M1 Abrams tank is more capable than a T54, and information on types is thus important for assessments of the significance of transfers. Moreover, measured by value, German exports would appear less significant, as many of its transfers were virtually

---

[14] *The United Nations Register of Conventional Armaments; Report of the Secretary-General,* United Nations document A/48/344, 11 October 1993. For an analysis of the first report of the UN Register, see: M. Chalmers and O. Greene, *The United Nations Register of Conventional Armaments: an initial examination of the First Report,* Bradford Arms Register Studies (BARS) No 2, Bradford University, October 1993; E. Laurance, S. Wezeman, and H. Wulf, *Arms Watch: SIPRI report on the first year of the UN Register of Conventional Arms,* SIPRI Research Report No 6, SIPRI/Oxford University Press, 1993; BASIC, *Moving Toward Transparency: an evaluation of the United Nations Register of Conventional Arms,* BASIC Report 93.6, London/Washington DC, 1993.

[15] E. Laurance, S. Wezeman, and H. Wulf , op cit

free, or at least low cost. In contrast, the UK's high value Al Yamamah arms deal with the Saudi Arabian government means that the
UK was almost certainly the leading EC exporter (by value) of arms
and related services during 1992.[16] Nevertheless, the numerical information in the Register is useful (and in many cases new), and Table 1
summarises the information on arms exports reported by EC states.

Table 1. EC arms exports for 1992, as reported to the UN Register

Country	Tanks	ACVs	Heavy Art.	Comb. A/craft	Helicopters	Warships	Missiles/ launchers
UK	31	46	13	19	-	1	446
France	-	36	215	16	1	-	26
Germany	140	136	449	18	1	19	13,540
Italy	-	-	9	7	10	-	8
Netherlands	100	81	171	-	-	-	

Other EC states submitted nil returns for arms exports covered by the Register in 1992.

Most of the reported exports from EC states were either transferred
to NATO allies or to recipients in the Middle East and the Far East - a
reflection of the fact that these areas are the three largest markets for
armaments. Not all of these recipients participated in the Register
themselves. For example, Saudi Arabia and the United Arab Emirates,
two of the biggest customers for UK and French exports, made no returns. However, using the data reported in the Register by EC and
other participating suppliers, it is possible to construct a reasonably
complete table of imports of major conventional arms by Saudi Arabia
and UAE in 1992 (see table 2). While this illustrates an important
strength of the Register, it was probably also a source of irritation to
the Saudi Arabian and UAE governments. As will be discussed further
in the next section, the UK and French governments are likely to be
sensitive to the views of such important customers, contributing to differences with several of their EC partners on the desirability of providing more detailed information on arms transfers reported to the
Register in future.

---

[16] However in 1992, the UK only reported the export of 1 combat aircraft, 29 armoured
combat vehicles and 48 missiles & missile launchers to Saudi Arabia. *United Nations Register of
Conventional Arms:Report of the Secretary General*, General Assembly Document A/48/344, pp.
105-106.

Table 2 Information in the Register on Imports of Saudi Arabia
and United Arab Emirates

Importer	Reported Exports to Importer	Exporter
Saudi Arabia	192 ACVs, 10 combat aircraft	USA
	29 ACVs, 1 combat aircraft	UK
	48 missiles/missile launchers	UK
	175 heavy artillery	France France
	6 missiles/missile launchers	Brazil
	50,328 artillery (SS30, SS40,	
	and SS60 rockets)	Canada
	262 ACVs	
United Arab	80 ACV	Russia
Emirates	398 missiles/missile launchers 6	UK
	ACVs	France

EC members were also confirmed to be amongst the major arms importers. According to the Register, Greece was amongst the two top importers in the world in 1992 (together with Turkey). This was largely a reflection of the "cascading" by NATO states to their less well-equipped allies of surplus (and mostly relatively old) military equipment which might otherwise have been destroyed under the CFE, enhanced by similar transfers of equipment released as a consequence of budgetary cuts in armed forces. Table 3 summarises the information on arms imports reported by EC states.

In this context, it is noteworthy that, although EC states have aimed to coordinate their participation in the register, they have adopted differing policies in relation to providing information about weapons types in their reports of arms transfers. In the standardised form on arms transfers which participating states should complete, there are two "remarks" columns,

Table 3. E.C. States Imports of Major Conventional Arms in 1992,
As Reported in the UN Register

Country	Tanks	ACVs	Heavy Artillery	Comb, Aircraft	Heli-copters	War-ships	Missiles/ missile launchers
Belgium	2	2	2	2	10		
Denmark		25					2
Germany							4
Greece	592	206	243	33		13	128
Italy			2				8
Netherlands				2			
Portugal		26					13
Spain	96						11
UK	1	10	18				7,778

Note: The remaining EC states submitted nil returns

where states are invited to describe the items transferred and make comments on the transfer. Completion of these is left entirely to the discretion of the participating state. Globally, 33 states chose to include details of weapon types in their reports of arms transfers in 1992, out of a total of 44 participating countries that reported arms transfers (the remainder of participating states either reported nil returns, or did not complete their forms). In the EC, Germany, Greece, Italy, Netherlands, Portugal and Spain provided details of weapon types; whereas France, UK, Belgium, and Denmark did not (Ireland and Luxembourg made nil returns).

Notably, the UN Register included information on a substantial number of transfers that had not been picked up by independent "arms watchers" such as SIPRI. This was particularly the case for land systems such as ACVs and heavy artillery. For example, all of the exports of ACVs in 1992 reported by France (and all but one of those reported by the UK) were not included in the SIPRI database. In many other cases, there were substantial differences between the numbers reported by SIPRI and in the UN Register.[17]

Where both importers and exporters reported on the same transfer, it is possible to cross-check the reported import and export data contained in the Register. In this way, for example, the German report cast significant light on some transfers contained in the UK submission: whereas the UK simply reported that it imported 6888 missiles and missile launchers from Germany in 1992, the German report identifies these as 6888 RP/C M-26 rockets for the MLRS. [18] Thus, some EC states' policies had the effect of increasing the transparency of other members' transfer activities. This reflects the fact that EC states were unable to agree a coordinated policy for providing further information on weapon designations in their register returns for 1992.

As was common throughout the Register in its first year of operation[19], the data provided by EC states often did not match with that provided by its trading partner. For example, Greece reported receiving only 347 of the 492 tanks that the US reported exporting to it. Such discrepancies often seemed to reflect differences in interpretation of the requirements of the Register or differences in national data collection methodologies.

Hopefully, these are largely "teething" problems that will be less significant in future years. However, it does illustrate the fact that even countries with relatively well-developed national systems for monitoring and controlling arms transfers (and most EC states would

---

[17] See E. Laurance, S. Wezeman, and H. Wulf , op cit, for a detailed comparison of SIPRI data and the UN Register.

[18] An example noted, for example, in E. Laurance, S. Wezeman and H. Wulf, op cit, p33.

[19] As discussed in M. Chalmers and O. Greene, op cit; and E. Laurance et al, op cit.

claim to be amongst these) experienced real difficulties in compiling their submissions to the Register. Most states have not previously monitored their annual arms imports and exports (concentrating instead on export licenses, for example, which usually provide little indication of which year a transfer will take place, or even whether it takes place at all).

In contrast to the division within the EC relating to providing information on weapons types, EC states adopted a relatively unified and positive approach to providing "background information" on their national holdings of military equipment and military procurement in 1992. Globally, only 21 of the states participating in the Register in its first year of operation provided background information on holdings and procurement, and nearly all of these were western CSCE members (Bulgaria, Hungary, Poland, Japan, Brazil, Chile, and Nicaragua were the others). However, within the EC, only Ireland and Luxemburg did not report such information.

This relative willingness to report information on holding and procurement is probably largely a reflection of their involvement in the CFE treaty and in CSCE transparency regimes. These regimes require member states to exchange detailed information on military holdings (including details of equipment type and their location in the CFE Treaty). In this context, it is a relatively small step for these states to provide such information for the Register. For this reason, there is a reasonable prospect that many of the remaining CSCE states will provide background information on holdings and procurement to the Register in 1994, although the attitudes of Russia and other Soviet successor states remain very uncertain.

An important aim of the UN Register is to improve transparency so as to promote international and domestic pressures for restraint in engaging in potentially destabilising arms transfers. In this context, the question of the extent to which information provided in the register is made publically available is an important one. EC countries are relatively open societies, but they still leave much to be desired in their practices of providing timely information on arms transfers to their national legislatures or their publics. Although the annual report of the UN Register is published (though reported background information on holdings and procurement is not included in this report), most EC states did not publish their submissions at the same time as they sent them to the Office of Disarmament Affairs in New York. In the UK, for example, the UK's submission for the Register was lodged in the libraries of the Houses of parliament, but there was real uncertainty amongst relevant officials about the extent to which the information in the UK's own report could be freely circulated, let alone the information in other EC countries' submissions. There are proposals that CSCE states should in future exchange their submissions for the Register amongst themselves at the same time as they are sent to the ODA. While this would be a welcome development, it would be preferable if the reports were simply openly published, so as to increase public access to the information contained within them. EC states could take a lead in this by agreeing to do this themselves next year.

THE EC AND THE FUTURE DEVELOPMENT OF THE UN REGISTER

The immediate issue for EC states in relation to the future development of the Register is their policy towards the 1994 review process. The 1994 UN Group of Governmental Experts met for the first time in February 1994, and is due to report by September 1994. France, Germany, the Netherlands and the UK are present on the 23 member Group, and the Dutch representative Mr Wagenmakers has once again been appointed as Chair. The task of the Group is to report on the implementation of the Register and on ways in which it should be developed after 1994. At the top of its agenda is how (and whether) to extend the Register to include military holdings and procurement from national production. It is also considering proposals for revising and adding categories of armaments or military systems covered by the Register and ways in which the usefulness and reliability of the Register could be improved.[20]

Since nearly all EC states provided background information on military holdings or procurement in their submissions to the Register, it seems reasonable to assume that they will be relatively sympathetic to proposals to extend the Register to cover procurement from national production and holdings. However, such an extension would raise many complex technical issues, and it is likely to be resisted by a number of non-EC states, particularly developing states with a substantial arms industry and relatively unfamiliar with transparency in these areas. In fulfilling their role as leading sponsors of the UN Register, EC states will have to balance the advantages of including procurement from national production and holdings fully in the Register with the risk of deterring wider participation in the Register by extending it too rapidly. India and China, for example, are reportedly reluctant to extend the coverage of the Register in this way. However, it is widely agreed that extending the Register at least to cover procurement from national production is important if the regime is to maintain its mo-

---

[20] The issues associated with developing the UN Register in line with this agenda is discussed in M. Chalmers and O. Greene, *Implementing and Developing the United Nations Register of Conventional Arms*, Peace Research Reports, No. 32, Bradford University, Bradford UK, May 1993.

mentum. In this way, the success of the 1994 review process will depend substantially on the willingness of EC states (and particularly of countries represented on the panel) to overcome political resistance to extending the Register in this way.

On the question of revising the categories of equipment covered by the Register, and increasing the information provided on arms transfers (including weapons types), EC states are likely to be divided amongst themselves. At the beginning of the 1994 review process, France and UK were resistant to providing details of weapon types (particularly in the category of missiles and missile launchers), while the Netherlands and Germany supported such a measure. EC states and their associates had not yet reached a common position on proposals to revise existing categories (such as whether to reduce the threshold of including warships from 750 tonnes, including all military training aircraft in the combat aircraft category, and dividing the missile & missile launchers category into two separate categories (missiles and RPVs, and missile launchers).

Another dimension of the further development of the Register is to widen participation. Three regions of the world where this is critical are the Middle East, the Far East, and Africa. In all of these regions, EC states are in position to exert significant influence and to lobby countries that did not participate in the first year of the Register to do so in future (or, if they did not complete their reports properly for 1992, to do so). As discussed in an earlier section of this paper, such EC activities were important in establishing the Register in 1993. However, there is a danger that EC governments will neglect to continue with this, especially if the political profile of the question of restraining the international arms trade in general, and the UN Register in particular, is lowered.

There may also be a number of unilateral steps that are open to EC members and their allies to strengthen the role of the UN Register in shaping the international arms trade. One is to link the authorisation of export licences to participation in the UN register in some way. For example, EC states could agree that any confidentiality clauses in arms transfer contracts should not limit full participation in the UN Register in any way. In the future, when the Register has become more established, they could link the granting of export licences for military equipment to whether the recipient states participate in the UN Register (using the UN Register as a minimal indication of that country's concern to promote regional security). Because of the competitiveness of the international arms trade, individual EC states would be reluctant to take such steps on their own. However, together, and if possible in concert with the USA and other non-EC suppliers, such measures are a real possibility.

CONCLUSION

The UN Register of Conventional Arms cannot be expected to have an immediate or major impact on the international arms trade or EC states' participation in it. It is designed to promote transparency rather than to regulate or enforce restraint. For the forseeable future it will focus on a limited number of categories of major weapons systems and weapons launchers, and will not cover small arms, military subsystems, arms production facilities or dual-technologies.

Nevertheless, transparency arrangements and CSBMs can contribute to promoting restraint in arms transfers, production and holdings, and to regional security. The EC has thus a long term security interest in the development of effective international transparency regimes and regional CSBMs. This implies a continuing interest in the health and further development of the UN Register, which has the potential to develop into an important transparency regime in its own right and also to provide a basis for the development of regional CSBMs in areas where they are presently inadequate (such as the Middle East, South Asia, the Asia-Pacific and Africa). The EC has played a leading role in developing the Register to this point, both in terms of promoting the establishment and development of the Register in the UN, and of encouraging wide participation in the register's first year of operation. However, the Register is still at an early (and fragile) stage of development, and depends substantially on the continuing and active support of EC states (amongst others).

Finally, in at least one crucial respect, the UN Register constitutes an improvement on CSCE transparency arrangements. Whereas CSBMs within the CSCE involve almost exclusively confidential intergovernmental exchanges of information on conventional forces, the public will have access to the information contained in the Register. Such openness is an advance on restricted intergovernmental transparency, and may facilitate the further democratisation of debates about arms transfers, procurement and holdings. The UN Register may therefore help to empower national legislatures and concerned citizens in relation to these issues, as well as provide a resource for the European Parliament. Both in its national and international effects, therefore, the Register provides a welcome addition to the family of transparency measures.

CHAPTER 7

MOTIVES AND THE MEANING OF GUIDELINES IN ARMS EXPORT POLICY:

THE U.K. AND THE IRAN-IRAQ WAR

Divina Miller

INTRODUCTION

All European states maintain that they have guidelines which govern their conventional arms transfer policies. While there is no uniformity among European states, such guidelines, or criteria, include: the existence of conflict; poor human rights records; involvement in terrorism; regional balances; and, of course, security. All of these criteria applied in the case of Iran and Iraq and yet Britain continued to supply both Iran and Iraq with defence equipment. It did so because of the importance of *both* defence and civil trade.

Arms are *controlled* because they represent the diffusion of strength in a competitive environment. At the same time, arms are sold because states inhabit that same competitive world. This is the difficulty which confronts decision-makers. This research suggests that for European states, as capitalist economies beset by the short-termism of electoral politics, the pressure to sell is in general stronger than the pressure to control save when the *immediate* security of the country is at stake. Guidelines are for public consumption not for private policy-making.

This case reveals the dilemmas for supplier states in attempting to curb proliferation. Iraq and Iran used the threat of disruption to civil trade as a means of acquiring defence equipment from the UK, and in the case of Iraq, as a means of preventing British interference in its procurement network.[1] This research suggests that the linking of civil to defence trade by would-be recipient states needs further exploration.

THE UK AND THE IRAN-IRAQ WAR

When war broke out between Iran and Iraq in September 1980, the British Government, having declared its neutrality, was legally bound not to provide military assistance to either side. The UK would not, it declared, sell lethal equipment to either participant. In 1984 this policy was apparently strengthened by the introduction of the following guidelines:

- We should maintain our consistent refusal to supply any lethal equipment to either side;
- Subject to that overriding consideration, we should attempt to fulfil existing contracts and obligations;
- We should not, in future, approve orders for any defence equipment which, in our view, would significantly enhance the capability of either side to prolong or exacerbate the conflict;
- In line with this policy, we should continue to scrutinise rigorously all applications for export licences for the supply of defence equipment to Iran and Iraq.[2]

The British Government instituted official machinery to execute the policy. Officials, like Colonel Glazebrook of the Ministry of Defence Working Group, toiled earnestly to implement that policy. Yet there is evidence to suggest that the Government subverted its own policy on arms transfers to Iran and Iraq. At a meeting between Lord Justice Scott and the Prosecuting Counsel in the Ordnance Technologies case,[3] the former remarked:

---

[1] See: *Inquiry into Exports of Defence Equipment and Dual Use Goods to Iraq*, Hearings in the presence of the Right Honourable Lord Justice Scott, Letter from Mr. Blackley to Sir David Miers and Minister for Foreign Affairs, 29 June 1988, read into the record during the Evidence of Sir David Miers, Day 19, 20 July 1993, pp.85-7; and, *Trade with Iraq*, Letter from the Secretary of State for Trade to the Prime Minister, 21 June 1990.

[2] *Official Report*, 29 October 1985, Vol. 84, col. 454,

[3] Three executives of Ordnance Technologies and a director of a transport company pleaded guilty at Reading Crown Court to charges of evasion of the prohibition on exportation

The powers that be knew that Jordan was being used (as a conduit for arms to Iraq) to some extent, yes. More than suspicion. They knew it was happening.[4]

The documentation underpinning his view is to be found, he said, in the Arms Working Party minutes and papers of the Defence and Overseas Committee of the Cabinet (DOPC).[5]

Some ex-participants in the trade in defence equipment with Iran and Iraq, notably Dr. Chris Cowley the Project Manager for *Project Babylon* and Mr. Gerald James the Chairman of *Astra*, have alleged that the trade with the two countries included lethal equipment and was conducted with the knowledge and even support of the British Government.

This paper, as an examination of *official* policy, is based solely upon: government documents released to the defence in the trial of the Matrix Churchill directors; the official papers read at the Inquiry into Exports of Defence Equipment and Dual Use Goods to Iraq; and evidence given to that Inquiry by officials and ministers.

This paper will argue that those documents show that the guidelines on defence exports to Iran and Iraq were not a policy for the war, and by extension for stability in the region, but a policy for two commercially important countries which happened to be at war. This was a policy that was not a palliative for domestic disquiet about the war and the UK's role as a supplier, but a policy that was meant to *symbolise* the UK's long-term position to both protagonists. As such, what was important was the declaratory policy rather than the operational policy. There was therefore no failure in control since the guidelines were a device for identifying those exports which, if officially sanctioned, would antagonise either side in the conflict. They did not constitute a system for identifying equipment which would affect the progress of the war.

That the UK's arms export policy should be driven by commercial concerns is perhaps not surprising. What is surprising is the absolute primacy of those concerns. For example, even the objections of the United States and the poor relations which the UK enjoyed with Iran during the 1980s served, not to change the policy of supplying defence equipment to that country, only to mask it.

---

contrary to the Customs and Excise Management Act in February 1992. An appeal has been mounted on the grounds that the Government knew that the fuze assembly line for Jordan was in fact destined for Iraq.

[4] *Inquiry into Exports of Defence Equipment and Dual Use Goods to Iraq*, Meeting between the Right Honourable Lord Justice Scott and the Prosecuting Counsel in the Ordnance Technologies case, 16 June 1993, p. 11.

[5] *Ibid*, pp. 8-9.

That the UK was driven by commercial concerns is revealed in the origins, in the institutional arrangements for the guidelines, and in the interpretation of the guidelines.

ORIGINS

> We were very good with words.
>
> Mark Higson
> Iraq Desk, Foreign and Commonwealth Office[6]

When war broke out between Iran and Iraq, Iran was already the subject of sanctions imposed by the European Community in response to the detention of American diplomats. Sanctions came into force with the Export of Goods (Control) Order 1980 of 29 May[7] but were lifted by the United Kingdom on 22 January 1981.

The UK had banned the transfer of all lethal defence equipment to both protagonists, but underneath this policy of even-handedness was a tilt towards Iraq: at a meeting of the DOPC four months after the outbreak of war, ministers agreed that:

> every opportunity should be taken to exploit Iraq's potentialities as a promising market for the sale of defence equipment, and to this end "lethal items" should be interpreted in the narrowest possible sense and the obligations of neutrality as flexibly as possible.[8]

"Lethal items" were interpreted as "military equipment designed to kill",[9] although no formal definition of "lethality" was ever drawn up by the Government to assist its officials in making decisions about export licence applications for Iran and Iraq.[10] While guns and ammunition were not supplied, directly or officially, some necessarily subjective judgments were made about all other forms of military equipment. For example, two ships, supplied by the UK to Iran in early 1984, were refitted with beds and operating rooms and called 'hospital' ships, although they were originally ordered as amphibious assault vessels and had mounts for four 40mm guns. A second example concerns an International Military Services (IMS) negotiated contract to build an inte-

---

[6] *Inquiry op cit*, Evidence of Mark Higson, Day 17, 15 July 1993, P- 95.

[7] *Bulletin of the European Communities Commission*, No. 4, 1980, Vol. 13, p.24.

[8] *Inquiry, op cit*, government document read into the record during the Evidence of Mr. Christopher Sandars, Day 3, 10 May 1993, p. 30.

[9] Mr. Alan Clark, Minister of State for Defence Procurement, *Hansard*, 2 May 1990, col. 603.

[10] *Inquiry, op cit*, Evidence of Sir Adam Butler, Day 6, 17 May 1993, p. 6.

grated weapons complex for Iraq. This was agreed with "the most swingeing Ministerial guarantee"[11] on 27 July 1981.

Communication systems and radar were exported and weapons training was regarded as "non-lethal". However, the most significant "non-lethal" export was that of spare parts, especially for tanks, aircraft and ships. This was particularly significant as far as Iran was concerned.

In attempting to disrupt Iran's war effort, the US Administration began "Operation Staunch" on 14 December 1983. The State Department instructed its embassies in countries believed to be transferring arms to Iran to encourage their host states to desist from the trade.[12] In February 1984, the Pentagon publicly criticised British transfers of spare parts for tanks and aircraft to Iran warning that even small items could be "incredibly helpful".[13] In July of the same year, the US again criticised the UK for continuing to supply Iran with "non-lethal" defence equipment,[14] and when the Prime Minister visited Washington in early 1985, she was urged to withhold arms transfers to Iran.[15] The new guidlines were perhaps meant to be the means od defence she took with her.

The then Head of Defence Secretariat 13 remembered that the guidelines were in part a response to American concerns about the refurbishment of British-supplied hovercraft and the supply of Olympus gas turbine engines for British-built frigates for Iran.[16] Others also emphasised American lobbying:

> The Americans had thrown in their lot with Iraq. The Arabs had always been very pro Iraq. We were coming under intense pressure really to abandon Iran altogether.[17]

Mr. Collins, Desk Officer for Iran in the Foreign and Commonwealth Office recalls "a major series of exchanges with the Americans".[18] In a note from Sir Richard Luce, Minister of State at the Foreign and Commonwealth Office, to Sir Adam Butler, Minister of State

---

[11] *Ibid*, Evidence of Sir Stephen Egerton, Day 11, 15 June 1993, pp. 82-3.

[12] *Report of the Congressional Committees Investigating the Iran-Contra Affair*, H. Rept. No. 100-433, 100th Congress, First Session, S.Rept. No. 100-216, Washington D.C., US Government Printing Office, 1987.

[13] *The Guardian*, 23 February 1984.

[14] *The Sunday Times*, 19 August 1984.

[15] United States, Department of State, "Iran-Iraq War (Discussion Points for Visit of Prime Minister Thatcher)", *National Security Archive Document 64218*, 12 December 1984.

[16] *Inquiry, op cit*, Evidence of Mr. Christopher Sandars, Day 3, 10 May 1993, p. 52.

[17] *Ibid, p.* 54.

[18] *Ibid*, Evidence of Mr. Collins, Day 10, 11 June 1993, p. 85.

for Defence Procurement (MSDP), the former refers to pressure from both the Americans and Iraq's friends in the Arab world.[19]

The Government in reviewing its arms export policy to Iran and Iraq had three choices: "abandon Iran altogether"; institute a total embargo; or keep or modify the existing policy.

The first was little discussed. Sir Adam Butler wrote of Iran at the time:

> We would not wish to totally sever the residual defence links which we have with her....it is important that relations of a more general sort are maintained with her.[20]

While the Americans and Arab states were concerned that Iran was making significant gains in the Gulf War, this alarm does not seem to have been shared by the UK.[21]

Honouring the existing contracts with Iran was seen as necessary in order "to be able to restore good relations both politically and from the commercial point of view as well".[22] There are, however, more references to the *commercial*, rather than the political, importance of Iran to the UK. Sir Richard Luce, initially a supporter of a complete embargo, emphasised the contractual obligations to Iran under the Shah and the consequences of not fulfilling them: "we would be liable to compensate British industry to many millions of pounds".[23]

Hence, the second guideline - the fulfilment of existing contracts - would allow trade with Iran to continue in the face of US and Arab pressure.

There was some discussion of instituting a total embargo, (on the initiative of the Foreign and Commonwealth Office), but this option was dismissed. While it would resolve the issue of American and Arab pressure to cease trading with Iran, it would antagonise Iraq and its supporters. Iraq, however, wanted the UK to do more to support its war effort:

> ....the Iraqi regime, with whom Britain at the time had considerable nonmilitary - ordinary commercial - relations were very irritated with us in Britain for not following other nations, Arab and non-Arab nations, in selling arms to them.[24]

---

[19] *Ibid,* government document read into the record during the Evidence of Sir Adam Butler, Day 6, 17 May 1993, p. 18.

[20] *Ibid, p.* 40.

[21] *Ibid,* FCO document, 24 October 1984, read into the record during the Evidence of Sir Stephen Egerton, Day 11, 15 June 1993, pp. 27-28.

[22] *Ibid,* Evidence of Sir Richard Luce, Day 1, 4 May 1993, p. 4.

[23] *Ibid,* pp. 7-8.

[24] *Ibid,* Evidence of Sir Richard Luce, Day 1, 4 May 1993, pp. 32-3.

More importantly, Iraq's Arab supporters influenced the decision not to institute a total embargo:

....we had important defence obligations towards them....in the general sense of contracts and training commitments, and, therefore, they took a very keen interest in our policy and particularly the possibility of there becoming any sort of arms embargo.[25]

Of more immediate and significant concern was "Saudi Arabia with whom we were just about to conclude, or had concluded, a very large contract for the sale of Tornado aircraft".[26] Colonel Glazebrook recalled that "we were being made to understand that Saudi Arabia was much more of a friend to the UK than was either Iran or Iraq".[27]

Thus the third guideline - the only new part of the UK's policy -was introduced to appease American and Arab concerns about Iraq's apparently faltering war effort. Sir Richard Luce wrote to the Head of the Middle East Department in December 1984:

Although there are new guidelines largely concerned with the presentation of policy, they also represent a modification of the substance of that policy....They are more acceptable to Arab countries and the US Government. They will give rise to greater difficulties with the Iranians and to British defence equipment manufacturers on the other hand.[28]

As the Head of the Middle East Department commented, "There was a change, but not a major change".[29]

INSTITUTIONAL ARRANGEMENTS

> I had an uncomfortable feeling that there were things going on behind my back about which I was not aware.
>
> Lieutenant Colonel Richard Glazebrook
> Ministry of Defence Working Group[30]

The guidelines came into force when the Prime Minister endorsed them on 12 December 1984.[31] They were first announced to Parliament on 29 October 1985 by Sir Geoffrey Howe, the Foreign Secretary. Insti-

---

[25] *Ibid*, Evidence of Mr. Day, Day 1, 4 May 1993, p. 160.

[26] *Ibid*, Evidence of Sir Stephen Egerton, Day 11, 15 June 1993, p. 30.

[27] *Ibid*, Evidence of Colonel Glazebrook, Day 4, 11 May 1993, p. 103.

[28] *Ibid*, government document read into the record during the Evidence of Sir Richard Luce, Day 1, 4 May 1993, pp. 76-7.

[29] *Ibid*, Evidence of Mr. Day, Day 1, 4 May 1993, p. 177.

[30] *Ibid*, Evidence of Colonel Glazebrook, Day 12, 21 June 1993, p. 176.

[31] *Ibid*, Evidence of Sir Richard Luce, Day 1, 4 May 1993, p. 71.

tutional arrangements were put in place to scrutinise export licence applications (ELA) for Iran and Iraq. The chief forum for this scrutiny was the Interdepartmental Committee on Defence Sales to Iran and Iraq (IDC).

Represented on the IDC were officials from the Department of Trade and Industry (DTI), the Ministry of Defence (MOD), and the Foreign and Commonwealth Office (FCO), which chaired and produced the minutes of the meetings held more or less every month. Each ministry had an informal veto on the approval of applications and an informal right to refer refusals up to ministers. Summary records of meetings were submitted to FCO, DTI and MOD ministers for approval with particularly sensitive items highlighted.

While the DTI and the FCO represented their particular departmental perspectives, and while it was the former which had the legal authority to issue or refuse export licences, it was the MOD which had to assess ELAs on their "lethality" and whether or not they "would significantly enhance the capability of either side to prolong or exacerbate the conflict". This task fell to the MOD Working Group (MODWG) comprising: the Regional Marketing Desks for Iran and Iraq, respectively RMD2A and RMD2B, from the Defence Exports Services Organisation (DESO), (the Government's arms salesmen); and operational, security and intelligence staff from within the MOD. The MODWG was chaired by a representative of the Defence Exports Services Secretariat (DESS), the central secretariat for DESO. It was he who took the MODWG's recommendations to the IDC where they could be overruled. The final outcomes of the IDC were not reported to the MODWG.

The MOD Arms Working Party (AWP), in consultation with the FCO, considered preliminary requests to export equipment. Most companies use the system in order not to waste resources pursuing sales that will never take place. The system "is fairly definitive in terms of leading to an export licence".[32] For Iran and Iraq, it was the MODWG which performed this function.

Companies could appeal refusals via the Regional Marketing Desks. DESS was supposed to take the appeal to the Release of Military Information Policy Committee (RMIPC). In the case of Iran and Iraq, however, they did not:

> Instead, they had a very protracted period of attempting to resolve differences and then went straight to the Minister for Defence Procurement for a decision.[33]

---

[32] *Ibid,* Evidence of Mr. Christopher Sandars, Day 3, 10 May 1993,10-11 .

[33] *Ibid,* Evidence of Lieutenant Colonel Glazebrook, Day 5, 12 May 1993, pp. 57-8.

Informal meetings would be set up by DESS, sometimes including military experts from DESO who could oppose the MODWG's own military experts. Alternatively, an appeal would simply go on and on being referred to the MODWG or DESO would appeal to officers superior to those who sat on the MODWG.[34]

Within the MOD, therefore, the institutional bias was towards sales for Iran and Iraq. That is not to say that the traditional restraints on sales - military security, operations, proliferation and the transfer of advanced technology - ceased to be applied for the two countries, (although even here there were differences of opinion). It means that given: the double representation of DESO on both the MODWG *and* the IDC; a DESS Chairman who represented the MODWG's views to the IDC; and the way the appeals procedure was conducted, the institutional arrangements clearly favoured sales. Given that the MODWG's task was to provide an assessment of an item's lethality or its contribution to the enhancement of military capability, one has to ask why the Government's salesmen needed to be represented on a committee which was performing what was essentially a technical task.

Colonel Glazebrook's description of how he assessed the Matrix Churchill machine tools illustrates the point. One particular batch was capable of producing 500,000 155 millimetre shells. With information supplied from Defence Intelligence regarding the number of 155mm guns in each division of the Iraqi Army and the number of divisions engaged in combat, as well as the expenditure rates, Colonel Glazebrook calculated that the enhancement was insignificant. However, he characterised the machine tools as "lethal".[35] (Later batches of machine tools would be classed by the MODWG as a significant enhancement of Iraq's capability to prolong the war after Iraq's concerted attempts to procure related technology for an indigenous arms industry became clear.[36])

The fact that DESS, although the "regulatory or monitoring body",[37] is part of DESO does reflect the Government's long standing aim of increasing defence sales. The "disposition to sell"[38] is evident in both the general institutional arrangements within the MOD for assessing ELAs and in the particular arrangements made for the implementation of the guidelines. However, this bias is also evident within

---

[34] *Ibid*, pp. 54-5; p. 76.

[35] *Ibid*, Day 4, 11 May 1993, pp. 74-5.

[36] *Ibid*, pp. 150-2.

[37] *Ibid*, Evidence of Mr. Christopher Sandars, Day 3, 10 May 1993, p. 160.

[38] Martin Edmonds, "The Domestic and International Dimensions of British Arms Sales, 1966-78", C. Cannizzo (Ed), *The Gun Merchants: Politics and Policies of the Major Arms Suppliers*, Oxford, Pergamon Press, 1980, p. 97.

government generally and finds its expression with respect to Iran and Iraq in the IDC. Lord Justice Scott is worth quoting at length on this point.

> It is not easy to see why it was necessary to have an IDC at all except that...the IDC provided another committee where the views which would otherwise have been out of court, because the MOD operational security would have ruled them out of court, are given a second bite and can then argue, with whatever hope of success they have, ...for the licences to go.[39]

Institutionally, power was vested not in those who had to assess ELAs or AWP applications in terms of the guidelines, but in those whose task it was to promote sales.

INTERPRETATION

> Unless you write down a list of items which cannot be exported....you just give criteria of the sort that are in the guidelines and there will be grey areas.
>
> Sir Adam Butler
> Minister of State for Defence Procurement[40]

Over a five year period (1985-9), eight per cent of the total applications for Iran were refused. (See Table 1.) For Iraq the figure is four per cent. Iran accounts for a total of 2325 ELAs, Iraq 1788. ELAs for Iran thus exceed those for Iraq by 30 per cent. The total of approved ELAs for Iran was 1732, 193 more than Iraq at 1539. Thus, 12.5 per cent more applications were approved for Iran than Iraq.

Table 1 Number of Applications and Outcomes for Iran and Iraq, 1985-89

	Received	Approved	Refused	Cancelled/Withdrawn
1985				
Iran	259	218	10	31
Iraq	367	323	11	33
1986				
Iran	298	256	17	25
Iraq	295	272	6	17

---

[39] *Inquiry, op cit*, Lord Justice Scott during Evidence of Sir Adam Butler, Day 6, 17 May 1993, pp. 153-4.
[40] *Annex to Brief for Minister of Defence Procurement for the Foreign Secretary's Meeting on 19 July, 1990.*

Table 1 (Continued)

	1987			
Iran	593	405	61	127
Iraq	315	272	16	27
	1988			
Iran	607	457	51	99
Iraq	401	327	25	49
	1989			
Iran	568	396	71	101
Iraq	410	345	19	46

Source: Letter from the Department of Trade and Industry to the Trade and Industry Committee, *Exports to Iraq*, Minutes of Evidence, Session 199192, House of Commons Papers, 86-viii, p. 297.

Two notes of caution are necessary. First, the low rate of refusals for both sides can be accounted for by companies seeking clearances in advance of ELAs. There are no equivalent figures for AWP clearances for Iran and Iraq. Second, no values or items are given. Only for 1989 are values available.

However, these figures are not representative of the whole period since, in 1989, Iran was being treated much more severely than Iraq because of the *fatwa* on Salman Rushdie.

Table 2 1989 Elas Approved and Refused for Iran and Iraq by Value

	Approved	*Refused*
Iran	50 million	70 million
Iraq	130 million	20 million

No figures are available for the years before the introduction of the guidelines, however, one participant remembers that, one year after the introduction of the guidelines, "there had been no great counter reaction that exports had been frustrated".[41]

Although the Government released a list of items exported to Iraq between 1987 and 1990,[42] no such list has been issued for Iran. Only a partial picture of approvals and refusals has emerged.

---

[41] *Inquiry, op cit*, Evidence of Mr. Day, Day 1, 4 May 1993, p. 186.

[42] Trade and Industry Committee, *Exports to Iraq*, Memorandum from the DTI, Annex E, Memoranda of Evidence, Session 1990-91, House of Commons Papers 607, pp. 43-48.

Disputes, particularly between the MODWG military experts and defence sales, arose around guidelines (ii) "existing contracts" and (iii) "significant enhancement". What constituted "lethal equipment" (guideline (i)) continued to be debated as it had since the beginning of the Iran-Iraq War.

DESO tried to extend the definition of an 'existing contract' to cover contracts signed after 1 January 1985. Whether this was ever resolved is not clear, but officials "argued backwards and forwards".[43] This uncertainty meant that the Chairman of the MODWG argued, with support from the Regional Marketing Desks, that:

> Where we have granted a licence and (the company) had subsequently signed a contract....we should continue to meet the contract even if circumstances changed.[44]

Guideline (ii) did mean that military spares continued to be supplied to both countries as companies would normally be contracted to supply them over the lifetime of the equipment originally supplied.[45]

Whether Iran or Iraq benefitted more from the supply of spares is difficult to gauge. However, given the supply, before 1980, of major weapons and weapons systems, it seems reasonable to assume that it was Iran which did best. Before 1980 Iran had received from the UK: some 875 Chieftain main battle tanks, 250 Scorpion light tanks, a destroyer, four frigates, six landing ships tank, a replenishment ship, military hovercraft, Seacat naval missiles, 114mm naval guns, and Rapier and Tigercat surface-to-air missiles. The major weapons and weapons systems of British manufacture Iraq had received before the war consisted of 15 Hawker Hunters and two Herons, 40 Gazelle, seven Puma and seven Lynx helicopters and Milan antitank guided weapons.[46]

The argument that existing contracts had to be honoured was also deployed when it became known that Matrix Churchill machine tools, already issued with an export licence, were being used to make shells in Iraq.[47]

Also used, in partial justification for allowing machine tools to be exported to Iraq, was the argument that these goods were dual use items and unless contrary *evidence* was provided, the DTI had no reason to refuse a licence. The onus for providing evidence was placed firmly

---

[43] *Inquiry, op cit*, Evidence of Colonel Glazebrook, Day 4, 11 May 1993, pp. 20-1.

[44] *Ibid* .

[45] *Ibid*.

[46] International Institute for Strategic Studies, *The Military Balance*, London, IISS, 1980-81, pp. 42-3.

[47] Letter from Anthony Steadman, Export Licensing Branch, to Allan Barratt, DESS, 13 January 1988.

upon the MODWG.[48] This argument was assisted by the vague, or deliberately misleading, way in which applications were completed, particularly that part which referred to "end use".

The argument regarding evidence was also deployed in respect of other dual use items. Aircraft spares for dual purpose aircraft were therefore permitted. Spares for Iranian Boeing 707s, F-27s, C-130s were approved at various times in spite of the use of these aircraft in operations in the Gulf. DESO insisted that "of course they (the aircraft) would be used for civil purposes at all stages"[49] and since civilian aircraft were owned by the two countries, the military experts were forced to concede defeat.

The third guideline was obviously problematical not least because Iran and Iraq "were two very different countries fighting a very different type of war".[50] There were, therefore, "asymmetrical results".[51] Thus the supply of radio equipment did not constitute a "significant enhancement" to Iraq, because it had good communications, but did so to Iran because it did not.[52] Although Defence Commitments Rest of the World (ROW) provided the MODWG with assessments of the state of the battle between Iran and Iraq, judgments were necessarily subjective. Furthermore, the MODWG knew that Guideline (iii) "was meant to be flexible".[53] Even when the MODWG did conclude that a particular item would represent a "significant enhancement", it could always be second guessed by the IDC, aided - significantly - by the fact that these were subjective judgments and *ipso facto* open to interpretation. For example, an ELA for a Marconi Tropospheric Scatter communications system for Iran was said to be for civilian use but when the MODWG dropped the points where it was to be located on to a map, it was discovered that these points represented the main military centres in Iran. The MODWG was concerned that it would be used to "control operations in the Gulf against the *Armilla* Patrol" and that it not only represented a "significant enhancement" but also a threat to British forces.[54] The application, worth £40 million, was permitted, after an appeal by the company assisted by DESO.

This example also serves to show two strategies used by DESO and companies in seeking to export defence equipment to Iran and Iraq. The first was to declare equipment to be bound for civilian use, where plausible, (and then to put the onus for showing otherwise on those who

---

[48] *Inquiry, op cit*, Evidence of Colonel Glazebrook, Day 4, 11 May 1993, p. 96.
[49] *Ibid*, pp. 68-9.
[50] *Ibid*, Evidence of Mr. Day, Day 1, 4 May 1993, p. 162.
[51] *Ibid*, Evidence of Mr . Christopher Sandars, Day 3, 10 May 1993, pp. 43-4.
[52] *Ibid*, Evidence of Colonel Glazebrook, Day 4, 11 May 1993, p. 54.
[53] *Ibid, p.* 8.
[54] *Ibid*, Day 5, 12 May 1993, pp. 32-3.

objected), and the second was to emphasise, or exaggerate, the value of particular contracts.[55]

In an age of total warfare, the supply of any product is going to enhance capability. A line has to be drawn. However, if the guidelines were a policy for the war, then that line would have be drawn between civil and military equipment. No distinction would have been necessary between lethal and non-lethal equipment. All defence equipment enhances the capability of either side to prolong or exacerbate the war and "significantly", to state the obvious, is a subjective word. An additional element of subjectivity is added with the words "in our view".

CHANGES TO THE GUIDELINES

The guidelines were subject to changes in interpretation over the period. These changes could be "formal", that is "instructions in writing to do something different from the guidelines as published in Parliament",[56] or informal, unwritten. However, both variations were treated in the same way. In 1984 a ban on chemical warfare equipment for both sides was introduced. In mid 1986, ministers instructed officials to take "a softer line with Iran".[57] In September 1987 the Foreign Secretary directed that spares for the Iranian Navy were to be stopped because of its increased threat to the *Armilla* Patrol. By early 1989, this ban had been lifted. There is also a reference to a change in the guidelines for Iran because of "evidence of Iran's involvement in terrorist activities",[58] although what form this change took is not evident. Most controversial of all has been the changing of the guidelines in 1988 following the ceasefire.

At a ministerial meeting, in December 1988, the third guideline was amended to read:

> We should not in future approve orders for any defence equipment which, in our view, would be of direct and significant assistance to either country in the conduct of offensive operations in breach of the ceasefire.[59]

---

[55] *Ibid*, pp. 43-4.

[56] *Ibid*, Day 4, 11 May 1993, p. 30.

[57] *Ibid, p.* 37.

[58] *Ibid*, Memorandum from Colonel Glazebrook, MODWG, to Mr. Allan Barratt, DESS, 14 February 1989, read into the record during the Evidence of Colonel Glazebrook, Day 4, 11 May 1993, pp. 44-5

[59] Evidence of Mr. John Goulden CMG, Assistant Under-Secretary of State at the Foreign and Commonwealth Office, to the Trade and Industry Committee, *op cit*, Minutes of Evidence, 28 January 1992, HC 86-viii, p.281 and *Defence Sales to Iran and Iraq: Proposed Revision*, 20 December 1988

This change simply reflected the changed circumstances of the ceasefire. It was a relaxation of British policy. However it was not to become official policy, that is it was not to be announced because of public sensitivity following Iraq's use of chemical weapons against the Kurds. Officials and ministers were to "operate flexibly within the guidelines".[60] The revised guidelines were applied: in effect, only equipment that was essential to offensive operations was denied to Iran and Iraq. In March 1989, following the crisis in Anglo-Iranian relations caused by the *fatwa* on Salman Rushdie, the IDC agreed that:

> The more flexible implementation of the guidelines which ministers had decided to take since the ceasefire would no longer be appropriate for Iran.[61]

Ministers confirmed the IDC's decisions, but they agreed that "this need not in principle preclude all sales to the Iranian Navy or to the Iranian Revolutionary Guards Corps".[62]

MOTIVES IN THE UK'S DEFENCE EXPORT POLICY TOWARDS IRAN AND IRAQ

POLITICAL MOTIVES I: DOMESTIC PUBLIC OPINION

The 1984 guidelines were *not* a response to public or Parliamentary pressure. Concern about the use of chemical weapons by the Iraqis had been largely done away with when the Government introduced the Export of Goods (Control) (Amendment No. 6) Order which made licensable eight chemicals which could be used for the manufacture of chemical weapons.[63] Sir Adam Butler, MSDP, recalled that in 1984 and 1985:

> There were relatively few direct approaches to....ministers, (I probably dealt with most of them)....there were no Parliamentary Questions to myself on the subject....there were very few letters dealing with it....it was not a subject which was being debated in Parliament.[64]

---

[60] *Inquiry, op cit*, Memorandum from the Foreign Secretary, Geoffrey Howe, 28 October 1988, read into the record during the Evidence of Sir David Miers, Day 18, 19 July 1993, p. 113.

[61] *Summary Record of the IDC*, 14 March 1989.

[62] Letter from William Waldegrave, Minister of State for Foreign and Commonwealth Affairs, to Alan Clark, Minister for Trade, 27 April 1989.

[63] *Hansard*, 12 April 1984, cols 339-340.

[64] *Inquiry, op cit*, Evidence of Sir Adam Butler, Day 6, 17 May 1993, p. 27.

Periodically there were Parliamentary Questions about British policy but no Debates on the issue. In 1984 and 1985, there was no evident public or press outrage at the Government's policy of continuing to supply "nonlethal" defence equipment to both Iran and Iraq.

The guidelines were not then a palliative for domestic public opinion. The pressure to change the UK's policy came from the United States and from Iraq's Arab supporters and it was because of these pressures that an announcement to Parliament was delayed for some eleven months.

Occasionally, officials and ministers were warned to be careful about the "public defensibility of individual decisions".[65] One such occasion was after revelations of secret American arms sales to Iran.[66] Again, in August 1987, the UK sent four British Hunt-class mine countermeasure vessels and a support ship to join the *Armilla* patrol because of the increased danger to shipping in the Gulf from mines. Consequently, there was increased media attention paid to the *Armilla* Patrol. An FCO memorandum noted the media coverage and that:

> It would not be publicly understood if it were known that we are continuing to sanction the export of spares that were enabling the Iranian Navy to mount attacks on our own and other friendly ships.[67]

The Foreign Secretary's decision not to publish the revised guidelines in 1988 was because of public concern about Iraq's use of chemical weapons against the Kurds. The sale of Hawk aircraft to Iraq was vetoed by the Prime Minister because "public opinion was overwhelmingly against in view of the human rights record of the Iraqi regime".[68] Again, following the Rushdie affair, the IDC was concerned about the "major presentational difficulties involved in any large defence exports to Iran".[69]

Public opinion occasionally brushed against the Government's policy nudging it towards temporary restraint, but, the main thrust of policy was unchanged. FCO internal guidelines say that "close attention should be paid to the recipient country if such a country has a bad record of human rights",[70] but there are no references to the human rights records of either Iran or Iraq in considering export licence appli-

---

[65] *Ibid*, FCO Minute, 26 November 1986, read into the record during the Evidence of Sir David Miers, Day 18, 19 July 1993, pp. 94-5.

[66] *Ibid*.

[67] *Ibid*, Evidence of Sir David Miers, Day 18, 19 July 1993, pp. 102-3.

[68] *Briefing* for William Waldegrave's meeting with Minister for Trade, Lord Trefgarne and Minister for Defence Procurement, Alan Clark, 1 November 1989.

[69] *Summary Record of the IDC*, 14 March 1989.

[70] *Ibid*, FCO internal guidelines for considering arms export applications, 2 April 1984, read into the record during the Evidence of Sir Richard Luce, Day 1, 4 May 1993, p. 11.

cations except in relation to public opinion. However, even after "tens and tens and tens of letters about the gassing of Kurds and political prisoners",[71] public opinion did not change the policy: it merely made the Government more circumspect about *some* exports. Hawk was one such example for Iraq. A microwave detector for Iran was deferred following the Rushdie affair "because of the possibilities of public misinterpretation of the uses of (it)".[72]

POLITICAL MOTIVES II: INTERNATIONAL OPINION

The UK's arms export policy was conditioned, politically, only by its interest in supporting, or in being seen to support, *American* initiatives to maintain stability in the Gulf. The guidelines were not a response to the war: they were a response to US and Arab pressure, as evidenced in their origins. That the guidelines were aimed, not at the war, but at international opinion can also be seen in their subsequent interpretation. For example, Iran wanted to import small boats from the UK in 1985. These were considered to be a "significant enhancement". The IDC minutes of 8 January 1985 note that the Middle East Department "appeared to be against the supply of any boat or ship, even dinghy, to Iran because of the presentational aspect to America".[73] In 1986, Westland applied for an ELA to refurbish two hovercraft which they were using to resupply their bridgehead in Arab territory. The matter had to be resolved by the Prime Minister after the DTI refused to give way to the objections of the MOD and FCO. Her response was that:

> We must adhere rigidly to the normal guidelines in these matters. Not to do so would mean going back on the assurances which the Prime Minister has given on many occasions to Arab countries.[74]

A letter from Sir Adam Butler to Sir Richard Luce in 1984 argued that, in briefing UK embassies, "we should be careful not to give too much detail on what is likely to continue to dribble to Iran".[75] The guidelines were not announced to parliament and public for some eleven months because:

[71] *Inquiry, op cit*, Evidence of Mark Higson, Day 17, 15 July 1993, p.52.

[72] *Summary Record of the IDC*, 23 March 1989.

[73] *Ibid*, Summary Record of the IDC, 8 January 1985, read into the record during the Evidence of Mr. Collins, Day 10, 11 June 1993, p.73.

[74] *Ibid*, Letter from the Prime Minister, 19 August 1986, read into the record during the Evidence of Paul Channon, Day 7, 19 May 1993, p. 115.

[75] *Ibid*, Letter from Sir Adam Butler to Sir Richard Luce, 1984, read into the record during the Evidence of Sir Adam Butler, Day 6, 17 May 1993, pp 48-9.

If you state publicly that the contracts with Iran were continuing, you would be drawing attention to it as a specific in a way which was potentially embarrassing (to) HMG because of our relationship with the Gulf states and with America.[76]

The *declaratory* policy was aimed at the US and Arab states and was a means of masking the *operational* policy of continuing the supply of defence equipment to Iran. Michael Heseltine wrote to the Foreign Secretary in 1984:

I welcome your assurance there will be a private degree of flexibility varying and improving the presentation of our policy without radically altering its substance.[77]

The third guideline was a code. Deciphered, "significant enhancement" meant "Arab and American objections to the sale of equipment to Iran". The term was also useful in assessing whether official exports of particular UK defence goods to Iraq would antagonise the Iranians.

POLITICAL MOTIVES III: INFLUENCE

Sir Richard Luce recalled of British policy:

....the Islamic fundamentalists who dominated the scene in Iran were viewed as a very serious threat to stability in the Middle East, but nevertheless....Iran longterm was important in terms of our relations with that region. Without a robust, stable Iran in the Gulf there would be instability in the Gulf.[78]

In continuing to supply Iran with defence equipment, the references, infrequently made, to British political interests in Iran echo Robert McFarlane, in 1985, in suggesting that the US cultivate the Iranian "moderates" by, *inter alia*, supplying arms.[79] However, it remains to be seen what the purpose of such influence was, since Britain's political interests in the region were essentially limited. (There is, for example, no mention of the hostage crisis in the Lebanon.) This is not to deny the strategic importance of Iran nor to deny that the British Government *was* attempting to gain some leverage there. Given that some British

---

[76] *Ibid*, Evidence of Sir Adam Butler, Day 6, 17 May 1993, p. 63.

[77] *Ibid*, Letter from Michael Heseltine, Secretary of State for Defence, to the Foreign Secretary, 1984, read into the record during the evidence of Mr . Christopher Sandars, Day 3, 10 May 1993, p. 93.

[78] *Inquiry, op cit*, Evidence of Sir Richard Luce, Day 1, 4 May 1993, p. 5.

[79] Draft National Security Directive, "US Policy toward Iran", 11 June 1985, *The Iran-Contra Scandal: The Declassified History*, Edited by Peter Kornbluh and Malcom Byrne, New York, The New Press, 1993, p. 221.

businessmen act as informal agents for the Secret Intelligence Service, it is possible that the UK was attempting, via the medium of trade, to maintain intelligence. If this was the case, it is probable, because of the historical role of intelligence in maintaining close links between the UK and the US, that this was more a means of seeking influence with the *US*, whose Iranian intelligence operation had been shattered by the 1979 revolution, than with Iran. This, however, is speculation: the Government's own documents are replete with references to the *commercial* importance to the UK of Iran and Iraq rather than their political significance. The irresistible conclusion is that, if the UK sought influence, it was merely complementary to its real goal which was commerce.

POLITICAL MOTIVES IV: REGIONAL STABILITY

Sir Richard Luce defined the British interest in the Gulf as "to see stability" in the region. The Iran-Iraq War was thus seen as "very much contrary to the interests of the Western world".[80]

Ministers presented the UK's arms export policy towards the two protagonists as being related to those interests. Sir Richard Luce argued:

> ....the Soviet Union, France and increasingly the United States decided that they would give active support to Iraq in this war through supplies of equipment. We took the view, however, contrary to almost every other nation in the world, that we should have an evenhanded, even approach to the war, that it was *not in the interests of the Gulf that this war should be prolonged*.[81]

(Emphasis added.)

The FCO defined its policy objectives towards the Iran-Iraq War as:

(a) to promote an early negotiated settlement;
(b) to ensure that the waterways are safe thus to contribute to upholding freedom of navigation for all merchant shipping;
(c) to limit the spread of Soviet influence in the strategically vital Gulf area.[82]

---

[80] *Ibid*, Evidence of Sir Richard Luce, Day 1, 4 May 1993, pp. 3-4.

[81] *Ibid*, p. 7.

[82] Foreign Affairs Committee, *Second Report: Current U~ Policy Towards the Iran-Iraq Conflict,* Session 1987-88, House of Commons Papers 279-I, p. xix.

While the UK might well have had an *interest* in stability in the Gulf in terms of the free flow of oil and its commercial links to the area, its *power* to affect that interest is inherently limited. Essentially, the promotion of stability - the maintenance of Middle Eastern regimes, the protection of free navigation and the containment of Soviet influence - was a task which fell to the Americans to perform. True, the UK has maintained strong links with the Gulf, a region in which it had only recently - 1971 - relinquished a permanent presence and Treaties of Friendship exist between the UK and Qatar, the United Arab Emirates and Bahrain. Defence relations with Kuwait, Oman and Saudi Arabia are described by the FCO as "close".[83] But, it is to the United States that the pro-Western regimes look when their security is threatened. The UK can only support the US. It cannot affect the course of events independently. Thus, the UK's interest in stability, in as much as interests are necessarily defined by power, is a modest one.

Similarly, the UK was unable to affect the progress of the war -its prolongation or its termination - because it lacked the resources to do so. (It could of course be argued that no state had the power to stop the Iran Iraq War, given the ideological commitment of Iran and its reliance upon infantry; that is, an arms embargo, proposed in 1987-8 to coerce Iran's acceptance of UN Security Council Resolution 598, might have been ineffective.) In any case, given the number of suppliers from an early stage and the involvement of the Superpowers as major suppliers, both before the war and from about 1983, Britain could not decisively affect the progress of the war either by supplying or withholding arms exports - she could only contribute. It is this lack of power, and the corresponding lack of interest, which made the UK behave without responsibility. That is to say, the UK, since it could not affect the war in any decisive way, was free, or compelled, to pursue its own real interest - commerce.

Thus, the guidelines did not address the issue of the war. When the FCO and the MOD discussed the introduction of the guidelines, they noted that "care would be necessary not to exclude sales of all equipment irrespective of their likely contribution to the prolongation of the war".[84] The guidelines, as the Head of the Middle East Department said, "were not intended to be a policy towards the war".[85]

---

[83] Foreign Affairs Committee, *The Iran-Iraq Conflict*, Minutes of Evidence, 10 February 1988, Memorandum submitted from the FCO, Session 1987-88, House of Commons papers 279-II, p. 27.

[84] *Inquiry, op cit*, Meeting between Sir Richard Luce, Minister of State for Foreign and Commonwealth Affairs, and Sir Adam Butler, Minister for Defence Procurement, 24 October 1984, document read into the record during the Evidence of Sir Richard Luce, Day 1, 4 May 1993, p. 35.

[85] *Ibid*, Evidence of Mr. Day, Day 1, 4 May 1993, p.169.

ECONOMIC MOTIVES

Defence sales are perceived to be economically important in themselves in terms of reducing unit costs, offsetting Research and Development costs and maintaining the defence base. Although these benefits are contested within and without government,[86] it seems clear that the Conservative Government, since 1979, has introduced mechanisms which give a greater priority to the export of defence equipment. Sir Adam Butler, for example, justifies the procurement and sales support as being together in the same department under the MSDP "because of the mutual benefit which arose".[87] There was, he said, a "general policy of selling defence equipment".[88]

However, the major economic motivation to sell arms, as far as Iran and Iraq were concerned, was to maintain commercial relationships with the two countries.

Iran, prior to the Revolution, had been an important export market for the United Kingdom. In March 1979, Chase Manhattan Bank estimated that the country would lose £500 million in export sales to Iran in that year causing a loss of three-tenths of a percentage point from its 2 per cent growth rate.[89] Iran was the United Kingdom's biggest export market for arms. While the Export Credits Guarantee Department had paid claims for losses by UK firms of £100 million by 1981, some equipment, already paid for by the Shah, remained in the UK.

When the Iran-Iraq War began, Iran was already the subject of sanctions. However, negotiations to resolve the pre- revolution contracts were continuing. In 1980, the UK was faced with two countries, oil rich and industrialising, which were both perceived to be of potential commercial importance. Iran had been the more important of the two, but the loss of the Iranian market had made the Iraqi market more significant than it might otherwise have been. The tilt towards Iraq in the early stages of the war reflects this. Sir Stephen Egerton confesses that this was "for commercial reasons".[90]

However, what is perhaps surprising, given the UK's, and certainly the Conservative Government's, tradition of loyalty to US policies, is the continuing trade in defence equipment with Iran. One can explain this by looking at the Government's own trade figures for the two countries. One sees that it is *Iran*, and not Iraq, which is of significantly greater commercial importance.

---

[86] See, for example, F.S. Pearson, "The Question of Control in British Defence Sales Policy", *International Affairs*, 59 (2), Spring 1983, p. 237.

[87] *Inquiry, op* cit, Evidence of Sir Adam Butler, Day 6, 17 May 1993, p. 3.

[88] *Ibid*, pp. 1-2.

[89] *Daily Telegraph*, 12 March 1979.

[90] *Inquiry, op cit*, Evidence of Sir Stephen Egerton, Day 11, 15 June 1993, p. 12.

Table 3 U.K. Exports and Imports: Iran and Iraq

		1983	1984	1985	1986	1987*
Iraq	Imports	30,334	69,047	44,125	66,129	33,871
	Exports	399,920	43,120	444,749	443,890	271,655
Iran	Imports	100,593	368,572	63,317	100,303	187,572
	Exports	630,683	703,384	525,589	399,373	307,853

£ *thousand** Years for which comparative figures available.

Source: Foreign Affairs Committee, *The Iran-Iraq Conflict*, Minutes of Evidence, Session 1987-88, House of Commons Papers 279-vii, 20 April 1988, p. 110.

At the first meeting of the MODWG on 13 December 1984, the record states that:

> Defence Commitments (ROW) said he had seen a reply from the Secretary of State, submission on tank engine spares for Iran, which stressed the need for officials to bear in mind the need not to prejudice civil trade while operating within the revised guidelines.[91]

This was a point, said Colonel Glazebrook, "that was made to us frequently".[92] In 1986, the MODWG were again reminded of the point in relation to Iran. At a ministerial meeting to review the guidelines, there was:

> A general agreement that in continuing to consider proposals for the export of equipment to Iran on their merits and against the guidelines, one of the factors that needed to be borne in mind was the importance of retaining long-term trading relations with Iran.[93]

This decision was communicated to officials, including the MODWG.[94]

Of greater commercial importance than both Iran and Iraq was Saudi Arabia and the other Gulf states. The guidelines were aimed at these markets both in formulation and in execution. The export of small boats to Iran was blocked because:

---

[91] *Ibid*, Record of the MODWG, 13 December 1984, read into the record during the Evidence of Colonel Glazebrook, Day 4, 11 May 1993, p. 29.

[92] *Ibid*.

[93] *Ibid*, Minute of a ministerial meeting to review the guidelines, read into the record during the Evidence of Colonel Glazebrook, Day 4, 11 May 1993, p. 36.

[94] *Ibid*, Evidence of Colonel Glazebrook, Day 4, 11 May 1993, p. 37.

The real argument against supply is that the Saudis and perhaps the Americans will object and the Tornado financing package could be jeopardised.[95]

However, the arguments were "finely balanced". It was also contended that:

We should not accept the Saudi veto when Iran is suddenly looking interesting again and making overtures.[96]

That the arguments over particular sales were finely balanced reflects the state of the UK's commercial interests in the Gulf.

When the guidelines were reviewed in 1986, ministers concluded that they should:

...continue to ensure that due weight is given to the sensibilities of the Gulf Cooperation Council states. This is perhaps particularly relevant in consideration of the presentational aspects of any potential sale.[97]

The guidelines were introduced as a way of alerting ministers to ELAs for Iran that would cause anxiety to the Americans, and, more particularly, Saudi Arabia and other Gulf states. Their further purpose was to assist in the justification, to the US and the Arab states, of sales that the Government wanted to make to Iran. As Sir David Miers, then Assistant Under Secretary supervising the Middle and Near East Departments, wrote in 1986:

I believe the guidelines should be regarded primarily as the set of criteria for use in defending against.... criticism from the Americans and the Saudis, whatever decision we take on grounds of commercial and political interests.[98]

The overriding importance of commerce to the UK is also evident in the Government's actions when Iraq's procurement strategy became known to them.

The Secretary of State for Trade wrote to the Prime Minister in June 1990 to say:

---

[95] *Ibid*, Memorandum from Sir David Miers, July 1986, read into the record during the Evidence of Sir David Miers, Day 18, 19 July 1993, pp. 91-2.

[96] *Ibid*.

[97] *Ibid*, Letter from Lord Trefgarne, Minister for Defence Procurement, to Timothy Renton, Minister of State for Foreign and Commonwealth Affairs, read irto the record during the Evidence of Colonel Glazebrook, Day 4, 11 May 1993, pp. 38-9.

[98] *Ibid*, Memorandum from Sir David Miers to Mr. Collecott, Middle East Department, July 1986, read into the record during the Evidence of Sir David Miers, Day 18, 19 July 1993, p. 83.

On the one hand we need to minimise our involvement in the Iraqi procurement programme. But we also need to bear in mind the implication of export
controls on our exports to Iraq.[99]

That the commercial motive has gained such pre-eminence can be
seen in the coincidence of perception about the sale of defence equipment to Iran and Iraq between the three departments who would normally be involved in decision-making.

It was, of course, the FCO which one would expect to be the main
brake on defence exports. The FCO was chiefly concerned about the
presentational aspects of defence sales to Iran and Iraq to other states
as well as to Parliament and public. While Mark Higson argued that
the FCO "did try harder than other ministries to stop exports of material that we knew could be used for making arms",[100] Sir David Miers,
gave a different view of the Matrix Churchill case:

I thought the commercial and employment aspects of this particular sale
were important.

Q. More important than worrying about whether or not there was going to
be a significant enhancement to the Iraqis' munitions-making capability?

Yes.[101]

William Waldegrave, Minister of State for Foreign and Commonwealth Affairs, approved an ELA for a sonar research facility in spite
of the Minister of State for Defence Procurement's refusal. Mr. Waldegrave approved the sale in 1990 because "it looks as though we are just
looking for excuses to irritate the Iraqis".[102]

While companies, the DTI and DESO, given their interests, lobby
for freedom to export, the FCO's willingness to countenance defence exports suggests that such exports constitute the most important diplomatic coin in relations with developing states. Furthermore, the FCO
seems to have embraced the knowledge that for the UK, as a declining
economic power with a post-war propensity to run a balance of trade
deficit, the national interest is now primarily economic, rather than
political. That is, arms sales serve commercial not political needs: it is
trade not influence which is sought. The following comment was made
by a former Head of the Middle East Department:

---

[99] *Trade with Iraq*, Letter from the Secretary of State for Trade to the Prime Minister, 21 June
1990.

[100] *Inquiry, op cit*, Evidence of Mark Higson, Day 17, 15 July 1993, p. 9.

[101] *Ibid*, Evidence of Sir David Miers, Day 19, 20 July 1993, p. 52.

[102] *Ibid*, Memorandum from Allan Barratt, DESS, to Alan Clark, Minister for defence
Procurement, April 1990, read into the record during the Evidence of Colonel Glazebrook,
Day 5, 12 May 1993, pp. 90-2.

The British interest was usually set in a broader context, particularly the need to maintain the full range of civil exports to the region. For example, if Her Majesty's Government refused to supply a particular item of equipment to one or other belligerent, would that government retaliate by cancelling contracts with a range of entirely unrelated British suppliers? At the time this was seen as a serious threat.[103]

THE U.K. AND ILLICIT ARMS TRANSFERS TO IRAN AND IRAQ

Neutrality was described by the FCO as a "careful public policy".[104] Sir David Miers, commenting on the possible diversion of arms via third countries, argued:

We have to recognise....that the importance of this policy was partly, in fact, in being seen to be operating a policy towards the belligerents. It was a political message rather than one that was actually going to affect the war....The important thing from our point of view was to be seen to be having a policy....If a consignment succeeded in getting round that policy....it was not actually going to affect the war very much. Nor was it going to affect the integrity of our policy, unless we connived at it.[105]

The UK was engaged in a delicate balancing act, trying to preserve the important market of Iran, on the one hand, and the important markets of the Arab states on the other. Each official sale symbolised the UK's policy not only towards the recipient but also towards the other belligerent. Each sale, therefore, had to be carefully justified - as Stanley and Pearton noted, "arms sales have the unruly habit of shattering both secrecy and ambiguity".[106] The guidelines were a mechanism for exculpation not control.

Although one should not minimise the intrinsic importance of defence exports - the documents reveal that the larger the order or the more precarious the trading position of the company, the harder it was to resist approving ELAs - the UK continued the defence trade with both Iran and Iraq because of the importance of civil exports. Ministers and officials perceived that both Iran and Iraq could and would use the lever of civil trade to obtain officially sanctioned defence equipment.

---

[103] *Ibid*, Evidence of Mr. Day, Day 1, 4 May 1993, p. 194.

[104] Letter from David Gore-Booth, Assistant Under Secretary FCO, to PS/Mr. Waldegrave, 31 October 1990.

[105] *Inquiry, op cit*, Evidence of Sir David Miers, Day 19, 20 July 1993, pp. 29-30.

[106] J. Stanley and M. Pearton, *The International Trade in Arms*, London, Chatto and Windus, 1972, p. 17.

If both countries were able to use the lever of civil trade to obtain
"nonlethal" defence equipment officially, it is possible that they were
also able to use the same lever to obtain "lethal" equipment unoffi-
cially. Furthermore, given that the UK was motivated almost purely
by commercial factors, it is entirely consistent that the UK would allow lethal equipment to be supplied to both parties so long as it lacked
any sense of officialness. As Alan Clark said:

> ...I think there was a tendency for the trickier items (for Iraq) to be con-
> signed to Jordan.[107]

Fouad Ayoub, the Jordanian Ambassador to the UK argued that "it
was no secret" that Jordan operated as a conduit for Western arms to
Iraq.[108]

Much has been made of the supposed tilt towards Iraq. If this was
the case, although there is little evidence of it in terms of what was
officially exported, one has to assume that this was because of commercial opportunism rather than because of policy. If it was the case
that the UK was attempting to prevent an Iraqi defeat, then, at the
very least it willed the end without willing the means. That is, the
UK continued to officially supply Iran with defence equipment and allowed Iran to co-ordinate its purchases of most of its arms from the offices of the National Iranian Oil Company in London. Allegations that
major British companies participated in European cartels to supply,
inter alia, explosives to Iran are entirely plausible.[109] Such supply
would not have undermined the policy, neutrality underpinned by the
guidelines, because this was only a "theoretical position".[110] Neither
does such supply undermine the UK's interests since these are now narrowly confined to commerce.

CONCLUSIONS

It might be argued that the UK cannot serve as an exemplar of the
major Western supplier for two reasons. The first is that of the weak-
ness of the UK economy: exports are particularly important. The second
reason is the peculiar ideology of the Conservative government:

> The climate was 'free marketism'; and the foreign policy it gave rise to was
> a competitive internationalism.[111]

---

[107] *Inquiry, op* cit, Evidence of Mr. Alan Clark.
[108] "Special Assignment", *BBC Radio 4,* 30 April 1993.
[109] *The Guardian,* 30 December 1993.
[110] *Brief for Minister of Defence Procurement for Foreign Secretary's Meeting,* 17 July 1990.
[111] Bernard Porter, *Britain, Europe and the World 1850-1986:*

However, one can argue that if certain Third World states are able to pull on the lever of civil trade, then all European states are as vulnerable as the UK. Furthermore, the UK's arms export policy towards Iran and Iraq was only partly conditioned by the ideology of the free market: it was also governed by the UK's place in the international system. Only superpowers engaged in global competition have both the means and the imperative to supply or withhold arms for political motives.

This research suggests that factors such as the existence of conflict, poor human rights records, and domestic and international opinion, will be much less significant in governing the arms transfer policies of European states than the level of civil trade subsisting between potential supplier and recipient. That civil trade does not have to be substantial: Iraq represented half of one per cent of UK exports.[112] And yet that civil trade was important enough to not only permit exports of defence equipment to a state with a very poor human rights record and one engaged in conflict but also to inhibit action against Iraq's procurement network. Similarly, in spite of the same factors in Iran's case as well as: poor diplomatic relations; evidence of Iran's involvement in terrorism; and pressure from the US; the UK continued to supply defence equipment. Iran is the more noteworthy of the two countries, even though it was more important commercially, for all the above reasons *and* because of the threat posed by Iran to British forces operating in the Gulf.

The final conclusion is that scepticism about official arms transfer policies is necessary, particularly now that the structure of the arms trade has changed[113] and the mechanisms for the purchase and supply of illicit arms are so well established.[114]

Delusions of Grandeur, Second Edition, London, George Allen and Unwin, 1987, p. 146.

[112] Trade and Industry Committee, *op cit,* HC 86, p. xi.

[113] See Michael Klare, "The Arms Trade: Changing Patterns in the 1980s", *Third World Quarterly,* Vol. 9 (4), October 1987.

[114] See E. J. Laurance, "The New Gunrunning", Orbis, Vol. 33 (2), Spring 1989.

CHAPTER 8

EUROPE, ARMS TRANSFERS AND THE WAR IN YUGOSLAVIA: MORE THAN TECHNICALITIES?*

James Gow
Department of War Studies
King's College London

One week after Slovenia and Croatia declared their independence from the Socialist Federal Republic of Yugoslavia (SFRY) at the end of June 1991, the United Kingdom announced an embargo on the sale of arms to any part of the SFRY. This was soon followed by a similar ban imposed by the European Community in the framework of European Political Cooperation and the soon-to-be Common Foreign and Security Policy which was being drafted to follow. In September, the United Nations Security Council passed resolution 713 banning all transfer of arms to the SFRY, or any part of its territory. The embargo is a particular mechanism designed to control arms transfers. Whilst trade may be one aspect of the study of arms transfers, it is not the principal focus f an embargo, the aim of which is to cut the flow of weapons into certain hands. For this reason, trade is not considered in the following analysis. That is limited simply to the question of transfers - that is, the supply of military capability by one party, or parties, to another.

As the trouble in Yugoslavia has deepened and intensified, many questions have arisen in connection with the role played by such an embargo in a conflict of this kind. Some of these are of an entirely technical nature, concerning the ways in which the proscription of arms transfers is circumvented. Others are of a more philosophical and even

---

* Paper presented to SSRC-MacArthur Workshop on European Arms Trade and the EC (EU), Centre for Defence Studies, King's College London, 18-19 January 1994.

moral nature. Yet others, concern the nature of the European Union and the future of European security. The purpose of the present paper is to flag and discuss some of the issues which arise in relation to the control arms transfers and the war in Yugoslavia. Some of these are inevitably general and inherent in the question of trying to control the supply of arms to a zone of tension and conflict. Others, particularly those of a political or security nature, whilst essentially speculative, relate specifically and extensively to the European Union and the future of Europe. Analysis of this case can indicate (albeit sometimes obvious) principles concerning arms transfers, as well as signposting difficult questions in terms of European security.

ARMS AND YUGOSLAVIA

From before the beginning of the Yugoslav war of dissolution, the issue of arms transfers has been in question. To understand this means going back into the nature of the former Yugoslav state and looking at some of the critical factors as it approached breakup. In particular, there is a need to focus on the peculiarities of the Yugoslav defence system.

The federal system devised by Josip Broz Tito's communists after the Second World War to solve the nationalist problems which plagued Royal Yugoslavia between its formation in 1918 and its demise in 1941 provided the framework for embryonic states, particularly under the arrangements of the constitution adopted in 1974.[1] This gave considerable powers to the republics. That power was reinforced by the mechanisms of the communist system: in Yugoslavia, all power was in the republics, each run by a communist party with specific local interest. By the time communist rule ended in the Yugoslav republics, they were acting independently of each other and unable to cooperate for long enough at the federal level to carry out economic reform. The problems of achieving inter-republican agreement were accentuated by the electoral victories of governments of different ideological perspectives in al the republics, but each with a nationalist identity.

Another essential feature in any understanding of the issues involved is the old Yugoslav defence system. The doctrine of General Peoples Defence (GPD) in Yugoslavia developed a two-tier system of armed forces.[2] One part was the Yugoslav People's Army (YPA) a highly trained standing army based on conscription and run by the fed

---

[1] James Gow, "Deconstructing Yugoslavia', Survival, Vol. XXXIII No. 4 July/August 1991, passim,
[2] James Gow, Legitimacy and the Military: The Yugoslav Crisis, Pinter, London, 1992.

eral defence ministry. The other was a territorial defence force which would mobilize up to 85 percent of the population into a resistance force; responsibility for this was given to the republics. Thus Yugoslavia had one technically advanced federal armed force and a series of less well equipped republican-based armed forces. These became the basis for the formation of republican proto-armies as Slovenia and Crotia sought full statehood.

The YPA, aware of the role the Territorial forces might play, impounded virtually all of the weaponry designated for the Croatian force and about 40 percent of that for use by Slovenia. The weaponry involved include artillery, anti-air and anti-tank rocket systems (and rockets). Croatia, for example, and 200 of each type of rocket system and 9-10,000 rockets for each.[3] Both countries immediately sought to replenish their denuded stocks by making purchases outside Yugoslavia.

The only transaction officially reported was the sale by Hungary of 10-20,000 Kalashnikov automatic rifles to Croatia - and this deal only came into the open after a series of reports forced the Hungarian government to admit the sales.[4] Otherwise, equipment was obtained in, or from, at least ten countries. These included Austria, Italy, Czechoslovakia, Poland, Switzerland, Singapore, the two Koreas and Germany[5]; they also included some items of Yugoslav provenance rechannelled from Lebanese militias no longer requiring them. Secret arms markets in Austrian forests about 50 kilometers form the Slovene border were prime points of purchase.[6]

Secrecy was necessary in light of the difficulties all involved faced making deals which could not include Yugoslavia's federal authorities. Arms trade of any kind should have been subject to two federal laws - one on import-export business and the other on production and transfer of arms and military equipment. However, the constitutional status of the republican secretariats for defence and internal affairs gave the transactions attributes of legality[7]. Arms sales were not made, therefore, to rebel insurgents; they were made to appropriate constitutional entities.

Although many of the purchase ought to have been dealt with through the federal defence ministry, some republican defence acquisi-

---

[3]Slaven Letica and Mario Nobilio, Rat Protive Hrvatske, Globus, Zagreb, 1991, p. 72.

[4]Judith Patki, "Relations with Yugoslavia Troubled by Weapons Sale" Radio Free Europe Report on Eastern Europe, 22 February 1991.

[5]Borba, 15 January 1991, gave a detailed account of a delivery by a Czechoslovak company of 5000 pistols in Zagreb.

[6]Mladina, 4 December 1991.

[7]Stanoje Jovanovic, "Jasno definisian postupak premanja oruzaniah snaga' Odbrna I Zastita, Vol. XXXVII, No. 1, January 1991, p. 40.

tions, such as 4,000 horses (for pack work in mountains) form Poland, would not necessarily be subject to defence ministry vetting. Other items were disguised or imported in peces, avoiding the gaze of the defence ministry and not seeming to be objects of concern to those responsible for import-export trade. All this, including acts of direct smuggling, was activity conducted a haze of semi-legality: institutions entitled to buy arms did so form organisations entitled to sell them.

But, they either disguised them from Yugoslav federal agencies, such as the army, which, having already removed weapons designated for the territorial forces, could not be thought likely to sanction arrangements; or, they by-passed the federation for the same reasons. Secrecy was also a product of the awkward dislocation between the Yugoslav reality of states within a state and intentional principles proscribing arms transfers which would affect territorial order. For international purposes. Yugoslavia remained one state; internally, it had rally become several of them. To deal with de facto governments, those trading arms had to by-pass de jure authorities.

Following a deliberate strategy of buying only that which would be most cost effective and useful, particularly Soviet, American and German anti-tank and anti-war weapons, including SA-80s, SAM-7s and German armbrust anti-tank rockets. In both republics, liberal laws on hunting weaponry at both federal and republican levels also played a role. Licenses were plentiful for those wanting to take advantage of Austria's liberal gun law, where individuals could walk into a shop with a license form one of the Yugoslav republics and buy a wide variety of armaments. The biggest snag proved to be for those who were clumsy enough to try and bring fifty items at once without an export license; the Austrian authorities seized these weapons at customs. Otherwise, larger items were smuggled in pieces.[8]

These imports added to the enormous number of weapons already in Yugoslavia. In addition to the weaponry under the official control of either federal or republican authorities, there was an astonishing amount of personal firearms. In 1990, there were more licensed personal and private firearms in Yugoslavia per household that either motor vehicles or washing machines.[9]

MORAL AND PHILOSOPHICAL ISSUES

Once open hostilities had broken out in Slovenia and Croatia, for the authorities in those republics, acquiring arms became a greater necessity. However, both were able to use the armaments already at

---

[8]Mladina, 22 January 1991.
[9]Mladina, 4 December 1991.

their disposal to capture weaponry form their enemies. However, all discussion on Slovenia and Croatia pales at the side of Bosnia and Hercegovina. Whereas the former republics had some capability and , moreover, access to the Adriatic Sea and borders with generally sympathetic countries, Bosnia's position was different. Although some arms remained in the non-Serbian communities in Bosnia, these were mostly limited to personal firearms (there were, nonetheless, some armed Croat groups organised in western Hercegovina). The Muslim community, especially, was unarmed - in large part, the result of a campaign backed by the authorities in the republic and implemented jointly by the Yugoslav army and the republican interior ministry forces, to disarm and disband groups wherever there was the potential to create paramilitary formations.

However, in Bosnia, there was not only a stark imbalance in access to the armaments produced by the defence industry of the old state, but also a vital need for protection as the Serbian forces began to carry out campaigns of 'ethnic cleansing' throughout northern and eastern Bosnia. The aim of this policy was to create portions of territory which were ethnically homogeneous and, therefore, free form potentially hostile elements in the population. The practice of 'ethnic cleansing' involved massacre, rape, mutilation and torture and has been argued to constitute an act of genocide.[10] In this circumstance, the matter of a gain on arms transfers becomes critical: for the Muslims in Bosnia, let alone those from any other ethnic community who would fight to preserve the integrity of the state, the issue of access to arms was one of life and death.

This situation was one in which the block on arms transfers tot a war zone in which an overwhelming weapons imbalance existed and those with the preponderance of material were attempting genocide, left those without weapons unable to defend themselves and likely victims. The question at the heart of arguments on this was a moral one. Whether or not the Muslim population in Bosnia and Gercegovina had the humanitarian right, either to be protected by those with the wherewithal to do so, or try to defend themselves. Whilst various European countries, under the auspices of the UN have been trying to limit the extent of the horror in Bosnia through operations to provide humanitarian relief, the Bosnian Presidency and Government have persistently called or the arms embargo to be lifted in favour of the authorities in the country, arguing that the state and its threatened people should have the right to defend themselves.

All of this raises questions abut the extent to which attempts to control arms supplies should take into account local specifics before they are made reality. In the Yugoslav case, imposition of the embargo

---

[10]In

was a well-meant gesture, but one which does not appear to have been thought through to its full implications which emerged as the situation deteriorated. The effect of the embargo was minimal on the one side which had a preponderance of weapons and quite extensive on those without. As a matter of principle, it seems questionable to impose heavy restrictions, no matter how well intentioned those doing so are, on all sides in a situation where the sides are grossly unequal. There is small point in placing a blanket proscription on those who already have arms-a plenty and it is hard to defend decisions, effectively, to subject those without the means of self-defence to a similar regime, even though the imposition of an embargo may be argued to limit the intensity of the conflict.

There is a further sense in which the imposition of complete controls is doubtful. This is the reality that in Bosnia, especially or carrying out act of ethnic cleansing, it is not essential to use sophisticated weapons systems. The war in Bosnia, although significantly shaped by the possession of more modern equipment in certain categories on one side, is in no way dependent on modern weapons systems. The war in Bosnia, although significantly shaped by the possession of more modern equipment in certain categories on one side, is no way dependent on modern weapons. Technological advantage may be important in some senses - such as the Serbian maintenance of long-range sieges with heavy artillery - but it is generally irrelevant as ethnic cleansing has resulted principally form the use of personal weapons, often not even firearms.

Finally, the value associated with attempts to prevent the supply of arms is open to question when it is evident that, in spite of restraints in source countries and, even more, of considerable efforts by UN sanctioned forces tasked with intercepting and preventing the provision of arms to those subject to sanctions, when only certain weapons types are, in reality, under embargo. There are two aspects to this. The first concerns the relative ease with which the parties in Bosnia and those in neighbouring countries are able to gain arms. The second involves the types of equipment transferred, - a critical issue in Bosnia. The types of armament which would tip the strategic balance in Bosnia (heavy artillery and armour) are just the weapons types that it is hardest to smuggle and transfer illegally. It is these types of weapon which the Serbian side have possessed in abundance since the outset and which have the Bosnian Army has lacked. The Bosnian Government forces have, on the other hand, been able to acquire all kinds of portable weaponry - for example, a supply of 5,000 MILAN shoulder launched anti-armour systems, with munitions, which made a telling change in the fortunes of the Bosnian Army at the beginning of 1993, along with other deliveries of portable systems.

There are two points here. The first is that those weapons which would have most changed the course of the war were those which were really subject to the restraint of the UN embargo (although there are various practical difficulties which would have remained had there been no embargo, for example, delivery thorough hostile neighbouring countries). The second is that it is those weapons types with which the embargo could be breached that played the greatest part in violence against individual civilians and in actions to frustrate the work of UNPROFOR - hand grenades, mortars, various mines, automatic pistols and automatic rifles. The size and nature of heavy categories of arms, especially in the case of an enforced embargo, makes sanctions of this type of weapon effective. However, it appears to be relatively easy to transfer portable weapons, despite the prohibition.

TECHNICAL ISSUES

Any attempt at analysis of the technical aspects of attempts to control the illicit transfer of weaponry belongs in the sphere of classified information. This is even more the case when study condemns a continuing security situation, where complete restrictions on the supply of arms are in place and where forces of key European countries with an interest in arms transfers are under the UN flag, operating on a humanitarian mission in the midst of a war - as is the case in Bosnia and Hercegovinal. Without the opportunity to use such information, it is necessary to sketch in some of the technical aspects of illicit arms transfers in the context of Yugoslavia on the basis of those limited cases which have been openly reported. All parties in the Yugoslav war of dissolution have received arms through transfers in defiance of sanctions. At most, however, these, again, can only serve to highlight questions.

As early as September 1991. three Bedfordshire businessmen had been arrested in conjunction with an aircraft hangar full of arms destined for Croatia, however, the case was not further reported, There could be little doubt that businessmen in Bedford, Windsor and a host of other places around the United Kingdom and Europe were engaged in similar activities. Serbian intelligence and Mafia networks are believed to have a series of arms caches throughout Europe, especially in the Federal Republic of Germany, with operations such as Raven Gore engaged in a number of countries. However, those who would export to parts of the former Yugoslavia are to be found in all corners of the globe.

Weapons identified in Bosnia and Croatia of external provenance are probably too numerous to mention. In addition to the European collaborative MILAN anti-armour systems already mentioned, US Stinger anti-air rocket systems are to be found, as are Soviet (mainly SA-2)systems. Mortars, mines and automatic weapons have been identified with originated in the Russian Federation, Ukraine (Kiev was regarded as a particular focal point for arms deals involving all the parties to the Bosnian war), Moldova, the former East Germany, Poland, the Czech and Slovak Republics, Romania, Malaysia, China and Singapore, among others. In addition, financial assistance and political backing was important (which in the case of Bosnia came particularly from Muslim countries - Saudi Arabia and Kuwait gave money, Turkey political support and Iran was identified as attempting to supply weapons)[11] British and (West) German assault rifles have been identified, although these appear, in a sense, not to originate in their 'parent ' country (although there may be nuances to add to this - see below).

Austria has a key place in secret arms transfers, as was already identified. From time to time, advertisements with a Vienna telephone number, might appear in publications such as Jane's Defence Weekly, offering, for example, large quantities of former Warsaw Pact kit. With the Soviet retreat for Eastern Europe, the reduction in military commitment of the Central and East European countries and with elements of the former Soviet military falling apart in hunger and impecunity, there is a surplus of former Warsaw pact weaponry swilling around Europe. Operators in Austria, but also, of course, in other places, are able to act as middle-men, linking potential buyers and sellers.[12] Having established financial arrangements and completed agreements, the remaining issue is delivery.

There are two elements to this. One is provision of legal cover for the transfer, the other is physically to arrange delivery to the user. The provision of legal cover means forgery, or government complicity. Of these, the latter is the more effective. One example can begin to demonstrate this.[13] An Austrian citizen, Rudolf Breiner, living and working out of Marbella in Spain (in association fellow Austrian Peter Rohacek and Parviz Sigurdsson, an Iranian-born Danish citizen[14]), arranged for the transfer to Bosnia of 5,000 automatic pistols with ammunition, 25,000 Scorpion 7.62 combat rifles with ammunition, including

---

[11] The Independent, 22 December 1992, The Daily Telegraph, 25 January 1993 and , especially, The European, 24-31 January 1993.

[12] 2Mladina, 4 December 1990.

[13] This example is chosen as an illustration because there is, more or less, complete evidence for it as a result of an official Panamanian report and related prosecutions in Spain. The bulk of the following is based on Informe de la Comision Presidencial Para Investigar la Supeusta contracion de armamentos a nombere de la Republica de Panama, 16 August 1993.

[14] El Pais, 2 October 1993.

armour piercing bullets, and 200,000 Uzi sub-machine guns, reconditioned in Austria, plus ammunition.

It was officials in the Czech Republic, dealing with the application to export the pistols and ammunition from tow factories near Prague which disrupted Breiner's scheme. He twice applied for permission to get the arms exported. The first time, he was turned down straight as the Bolivian General whose signature was on the end user certificate produced was, the Czechs found on inquiry, retire. A second attempt was made using Panamanian end-user certificates for the whole consignment, that is, including the Scorpions and Uzis. Parts of the shipment were taken by waterway to Rotterdam, whilst others were said to have been delivered to an airstrip in a 'small European country.[15] The attempt to transfer was again stymied by the Czechs who, noticing the same names involved with the same consignment, but for a new destination, as the US to confirm with the Panamanians that the certificate was genuine - something for which there was reasonable doubt, given at the time, Panama was a country without an army, or a real police force which had just been invaded by the American military. The certificate was not - it had been illegally provided by the deputy head of the Panamanian consulate in the Spanish city of Barcelona (who, along with a colleague, was dismissed). The matter was subject to international criminal investigation and Breiner and the two others were arrested and later convicted in Spain.

However, in many cases end-user certificates are not as closely questioned and it is commonplace for the whole, or some part of a consignment of arms, never to reach the designated end-user point. In these cases, it is till necessary to arrange delivery to the point of use. Slovenia obtained assistance form the Pope for this in one case. Slovenian security forces proudly fly camouflaged Bell helicopters, purchased since the arms embargo was put in place. The helicopters were originally sold to the Vatican for transport purposes. However, shortly afterwards, they were re-exported to Slovenia and others purchased form the manufacturers on the grounds that the Pope and been an impeccable civilian user, one to overcome any doubts in that crucial grey zone of 'dual use' technology.[16]

Other attempts have been more obvious. Shipments believed to be from Iran have been intercepted. On one occasion an aircraft ostensibly carrying out a humanitarian aid flight was discovered at Zagreb car-

---

[15] The use of small airstrips in former Yugoslav states, or in neighboring countries, is commonplace - one such instance involving a Briton flying weapons onto a Croatian island, was reported in The Scottish Sunday Express, 3 July 1994.

[16] 6Jelko Kacin, subsequently to become Slovenian Minister of Defence, wrote about the acquisition f helicopters in Revija Obramba, Nos. 3 and 4, March and April, 1993.

rying Kalashnikov automatic rifles in September 1992.[17] A second prominent incident involving the aerial transport of weapons to Croatia occurred during the war in Croatia. In September 1991, a Ugandan Airlines Boeing 747 was forced by the Yugoslav air force to divert form its route to Ljubljana in Slovenia and made to land at Zagrev airport where it was discovered to be carrying 19 tons of weaponry shipped from the quasi-independent Bophuthatswana on behalf of the South African defence manufacturer Armscor (which was delivering as much as it could, being "unable to meet a request oft 26 tons of material of the shelf").[18] At other times, weapons have been discovered in humanitarian convoys traveling in Bosnia. The most obvious initial route to the former Yugoslavia is by water, either along the River Danube into Servia, or to the port of Bar in Montenegro, or to one of the ports on the Croatian coast. On several occasions, ships have been intercepted carrying weapons to some part of the Yugoslavia. One vessel. sailing out of a Greek port, was stopped in the Seychelles carrying arms either manufactured in, r being re-exported by, Serbia to Somalia.[19]

Behind all this activity, for it to be successful, there has to be assistance form elements in some governments, as was the case in the Panamanian example used above, or from the governments themselves and their secret services. A clear example of this was the identification of an arms consignment at Maribor airport in Slovenia in July 1993. The consignment, intended for Muslims in Bosnia, created a scandal for the Slovenian ministry of defence as the accompanying documents reported in the press indicated that not only had senior figures in the Slovene MoD and Slovene intelligence been involved in this operation,[20] but so, according to reports, had an intelligence officer, named as Dieter Hoffman, form German (although British sources interviewed stresses that he was a former officer, no longer in active service), who had been involved in flying helicopters with arms into Bosnia.[21] The presence of an officer of this kind raises a new set of questions about arms transfers and the war in Yugoslavia. These focus on the nature and future of the European Union and of European security.

---

[17]The Independent, 10 September 1992.

[18]The deal, worth 1.5 million, was planned by the Croatian Interior Ministry, with Armscor dealing with a Canadian-Croat intermediary, Anton Kidas, via a Johannesburg-based British broker. The consignment included 20,000 M-16 and 10,000 SK-47 rifles, 500,000 rounds of ammunition, grenade launchers and jeeps. The Independent, 17 September 1991.

[19]The Daily Telegraph, 6 March 1993.

[20]This affair was to produce a parliamentary commission of inquiry in Slovenia which was forced to extend its period of work as further detail were sought in July 1994. Republika, 16 July 1994; Mldadina, 12 July 1994.

[21]Vreme, 13 September 1993; Mladina, 7 September 1993.

EUROPEANS, ALLIES AND
ARMS TRANSFERS TO BOSNIA

The Alice in Wonderland war in Yugoslavia could be expected to produce a situation where soldiers from some European Union countries are deployed to carry out a humanitarian mission, but the intelligence service of one of their partners and allies may be involved in the covert transfer of arms into the war zone through proxies. Of course, it cannot be ruled out that agents form one or more of those countries with troops on the ground could be operating in this way. Quite clearly, however, aside form any practical questions of covert arms transfers, the issues of arms transfers has taxed the patience of those on both sides of an argument over Bosnia. Where some countries, such as the UK, have been opposed tot he supply of arms to Bosnia, others such as the Us and, in Europe, Germany, have strongly supported the idea of removing the UN Security Council sanctions on arms transfers.

Both UK and German companies have been implicated in arms transfers into the former Yugoslavia. Heckler and Koch, the German subsidiary of the UK's Royal Ordnance has been more that once associated with weapons identified in Yugoslavia and British SA-80 assault rifles have been noted. Whilst neither country, nor the companies involved, admits responsibility, it has emerged in the course the Scott Inquiry in the UK into arms sales to Iraq and in a court case taking place in Bonn, that versions of Royal Ordnance assault rifles have been delivered through its German subsidiary to Serbian forces.[22] On other occasions, Heckler and Koch weapons made under license in Singapore have been found in parts of the former Yugoslavia.

Whatever the position vis a vis the case of Royal Ordnance and Heckler and Koch, a more fundamental political question emerges. This concerns the development of Common Foreign and Security Policy (CFSP) within the European Union. Despite the maintenance of a common policy on the surface, there have been divisions among the members of the Union, with those whose troops are working with UNPROFOR tending to be cautious about using air power and lifting the arms embargo, whilst others tended to support those propositions, as did the US, which fervently advocated the policy of 'lift and strike'. To some extent, for those advocating arms transfers, the proposal was a substitute for taking action using their own armed forces: Bosnians should have been allowed t defend themselves because the US would not send in the Cavalry to do the job and other countries could not for a variety of reasons.

The quasi common policy within the EU, added to the split which occurred between the US ad nearly all the Europeans, especially the

[22]The Times, 18 January 1994.

British, where the difference over Bosnia were substantial and said to be more acrimonious that those of the 1950's over the Suez crisis, the much vaunted 'special relationship' notwithstanding, does not bode well for the future. This is so both in terms of the development and deepening of common policy in the EU and in terms of preserving the Transatlantic relationship which has underpinned security in Europe since the 1940's. Indeed, if the relationship with the US were to wane further, as sometimes seems possible in the light of further divisions on the question of arming the Bosnians, then the Europeans, if they are to have anything like an effective policy at all, will have to become more cohesive and coherent, otherwise decision-making will be too slow and cumbersome.

One of the critical findings of the international dimensions of the Yugoslav conflict is the following: the Europeans need US leadership; the US is not guaranteed to be there leading the way; even when it is present, it cannot be guaranteed to lead in the direction in which certain Europeans would want to go. The implication of this is that the Europeans will either flounder a little, or be required to share real common purpose and perspective on such crucial matters as arms transfers to Bosnia in order to make effective decisions. One may speculate that if the Europeans are able to move in this direction and are able to significantly to build up the Western European Union as a European pillar within NATO, then, whatever emerges (planning cells, for example) will need equipping. That could have implications for European defence related industry. Whatever happens in the future, it is clear that the question of arms transfers to Bosnia has provoked almost unprecedented friction between Western Allies. That friction would be so much the worse if the extensive engagement of one Ally's security services in transferring arms to Bosnia was identified.

CONCLUSION

The questions surrounding arms transfers to the former Yugoslavia, in some ways, are straightforward - tracing routes, identifying those involved in a network and assessing the qualities of dual technology. However, the issue of arms transfers raises other sets of problems, some moral and philosophical, linked to the question of self-defence, future ones in the realm of relations between the Europeans themselves concern the European body politic and the future of a Europe where allies and partners have radically different perspectives and friction emerges. Inter alia, debate on arms transfers to they former Yugoslavia, focuses thought on the future of Europe.

CHAPTER 9

ETHICS AND THE EUROPEAN ARMS TRADE

Barrie Paskins

The inclusion in this book of a chapter on ethics directs our attention to an important conviction which some people have an important scepticism that is harboured by man. The conviction is that arms trading is a deeply problematic activity that is all too liable to lead us into actions that are shameful, dishonorable. The scepticism is concerned with whether one can say anything "realistic" and "constructive" about the trade in arms. My aims are to show that the conviction is sound and the scepticism ultimately misplaced, though understandable. I shall argue that if we think clearly then we will see that there are sound concerns as well as much confusion in public unease about the arms trade. By the end of the chapter, I hope to have disentangled certain fundamental principles from a mass of indefensible prejudices. The principles in question do not resolve all difficulties and are no substitute for the careful export analysis of cases in other chapters of this book. They are principles which must be combined with prudence if sound judgment is to result. They are worth bringing to mind because it is all too easy for the complications of particular cases to impress us so deeply and so one-sided that we confuse the empowering concept of wee-informed conscience with the debilitating belief that only unprincipled pragmatism can measure up to the complexities of the facts.

Let us begin with a working definition of "the European arms trade". As I shall use these phrase, it refers to all sales and transfers of arms involving European states *except sales and transfers within formal public alliances*, such as NATO and the former Warsaw Pact organization. In distinguishing between the arms trade and dealing with NATO, I am following a practice which is well established in the literature. As we will see later, the distinction is well grounded in ethics. My exclusion of NATO and WPO sales and transfers is complemented by *three inclusion*. I take the trade to include all European states, east as well as west. I take the trade to be an activity that involves individuals, companies, trade unions, etc. s well as states. And I take the trade to include all relevantly debatable technologies, such as dual-capable systems and machine-tools whose likely use in the particular case is the production of weapons or dual capable systems.

This inclusive understanding of the European arms trade invites us to reflect on the ethics of sales and transfers by some but not all of the world's arms suppliers. "If we don t do it, then someone else will," is clearly a thought that will need our attention in due course.

A preliminary general discussion of ethics and realism will help us to keep the analysis within manageable limits. An aim of all responsible commentary, I shall assume is to identify the important realities without overemphasizing their true significance. The need for realism about what is truly significant has t be emphasized because ethical sensitivities are all too often engaged and exhausted by the superficialities of particular scandals. As other chapters in this book make plain, many shifts in the normative an institutional frameworks as the European arms trade have been the result of short-term responses to particular scandals. One of the proper demands of realism is that we strive to keep such things in proportion. A narrowly moralizing approach can be distinctly unhelpful in this regard.

The *ethics* of every aspect of international relations and of military affairs is problematic for many reasons of which two are perhaps especially worth mentioning. Because we live in a world of many faiths and of none we tend to feel that no normative starting-point can be assumed to be self-evidently authoritative, so how do we avoid begging the objections that others might have to our most dearly cherished values? And second, is this completely general problem not made all the more intractable by the widely held belief that war is essentially a clash of naked wills, an amoral enterprise that humanitarian categories are all too likely to misrepresent?

One possible response to these problems is to seek to locate the morality of arms trading in the waste of resources that it is said to involve. As other chapters of the is book remind us, the development of many countries has been impaired or misdirected by spending on arms and its concomitant enhancement of the privileges of armed elites. Whatever our values, it might be thought, we can surely agree that waste on these scale is deplorable. Alas, this simplistic approach cannot bring us close to the heart of the problem. No one but a complete and tough-minded pacifist would feel any confidence that all of the arms trade is a waste of resources. If there is such a thing as a just war or a just rebellion, then those who are to fight it need weapons, and it cannot be assumed *a priori* that it should be better for them to provide their own weapons than to have these supplied to them by established manufacturers. The pacifist witness is a vital part of every debate bout military affairs but the just war perspective is also indispensable. A stable programme of civic concern to monitor the arms trade requires something deeper than the preoccupation with avoiding waste. (Nor is it at all certain, let us remember, that a reduction in arms sales would generate wealth that could or would be better used elsewhere. It might produce nothing but unemployment!)

A second possible response to the problem of moralizing in a world of many faiths and of none is to avoid the issue be concentrating on the implications of our values, by asking what *we* can live with regardless of what others may think. Thus, one might try to tackle the issue of European arms sales by attempting to identify an idea of Europe, an ideal sufficiently rich in content and widely enough shared for "us Europeans" to accept its implications whatever others might think. Alas, a reading of the chapters on the is book on French, German and UK perspectives on the arms trade cannot but suggest that there is no such European ides. "We" are too divided on this matter for a communitarian approach. Furthermore, even if we could persuade ourselves that we are of one mind, the little fact of war's logic imposes a severe constraint on what I can make sense for us to think. War is a profoundly interactive undertaken, as Clausewitz constantly reminds us, and it is far from clear that any normative consensus, we as a community, might have can stand the strain of war-related interaction with people who see things differently. For example, if it were the case that we were especially discline to secret deals and government back-handers, the temptations and necessities of trade partners might make our high standards difficult to sustain. Something deeper and more universal,. if also by that very token more problematic, is required for realistic moral judgments about military affairs.

If we cannot rely on a European idea to guide our thought, then an obvious place to look for a suitable robust approach is to natural law, the set of universally understandable and universally binding principles which have often been thought to constitute the common conscience of mankind. Natural law is not without its problems, but it has the merits of a long history from which much can be learnt and an open-mindedness about what might be discovered by honest contemplation of other peoples' mores. Towards the end of this chapter, I shall try to show that it is indeed natural law that offers the obvious normative framework for thinking about arms sales and transfers.

According to the natural lawyers, principle and prudence are complementary. Principles of conduct do no apply themselves in complicated cases, but can be brought to bear only through the creative insights of people with the intellectual penetration and integrity of character to cope with the bewildering , frightening and exhaustion complexities of the hard case. (Natural lawyers also point out that many cases are simple, a salutary caution against the insider's tendency to evade public scrutiny by obfuscating simple cases.)

It is all too often supposed that there is an all-pervasive conflict between ethics and realism. The moralizer is thought to be a quixotic idealist; the realist to have the merit of looking facts in the face. Conflict and tension there may be, but it should not be overstated. Natural law requires an open-minded appraisal of all the factors that it would be reasonable to take into account in a given piece of deacon-making. It is thus in hearty agreement with one of the requirements of pragmatics. The natural lawyer is, to be sure, opposed to the tendency of some realists to think that all values can be reduced to something more objective, such as power or interest. But n this, many realist emphatically agree and with good reason. A true pragmatist cannot but keep an open mind about which values might prove to be important in a given situation, and should therefore \be chary of any attempt to dismiss all values as mere ideology. It is doubtful whether a complete pragmatist, who comes to every situation with a wholly open mind, is truly possible, for it is non-negotiable principle that puts the steel into tough politicians and civil servants as well as civic activist. Perhaps there are defensible forms or realism which take serious issue with the stern requirements of natural law, but it would be superficial to assume that there is automatic disagreement and in this chapter it is, I think, safe to try the hypothesis that there are principles on which the judgments of realist and natural lawyer may well converge.

Let us now turn from preliminaries to the European arms trade. It is usual to assume that states or governments are the principal participants in this trade. An earlier age when private companies were at liberty to make a good killing out of the trade is remembered with disapproval. A necessary first step towards ethical understanding is to look behind the land assumption that states or governments are primarily responsible. It is not impossible for the circumstances to arise in which individuals might very reasonably think that they have to take upon themselves, the onerous responsibility of supplying arms. The Spanish Civil War is a historic example of what might be involved. The powers that could and should have come to the assistance of Republican Spain in its struggle against internal rebellion assisted by fascist state aggression or intervention chose instead, to practice appeasement. Many honourable people found it impossible to reconcile themselves to this failure of states to discharge their responsibilities and took upon themselves, as individuals, to do the little that individuals could do to respond to needs which should properly have been met by the great powers. Those who joined the International Brigade devoted their very lives to protecting the Republic.

It requires no great leap of imagination t see that individuals might, in similar circumstances, very reasonably take the view that what is required of them is to provide weapons or training rather than military service. The arms embargo that seemed for a time to deprive Bosnian Muslims of the ability to protect themselves against the aggression of Serbs and Croates, enforced by an international community that allowed the aggressor to o unpunished while disarming the victim, readily lent itself to interpretation as a grave scandal of the sort that individuals might well have been needed to repair to the limited extent that individuals can the negligence of states.

Such cases are imprint as a reminder that the primary role of states in the arms trade presupposes that states are behaving properly. It is right for states t regulate the arms trade because it is states that have the power to supply arms when they are needed as well as to deny them when necessary. In this respect, the arms trade differs markedly form the trade in hard drugs with which it is all too often compared. States are the proper regulators of the arms trade not because the non-pacifist can safely assume that the trade should wholly cease, but because it is states that have the power and authority to determine where arms supplies are needed, as well as where they are not. When state are exercising their responsibilities properly, the question of individual initiative should not arise, Individuals are pushed into the picture by serious government failures.

The individual who thinks about whether states have failed so badly that the individual action is needed, faces very great difficulties for reasons which are wee understood, within the traditions of natural law. The state is relatively well placed to make well-informed prudent judgments about such serious matters as the supply of arms; the individual is ill-equipped.

The state's sources of information are likely to be much more copious and the state's many responsibilities and internal complexity should ensure that many factors are weighed against one another, whereas it is all too easy for individuals to rush to one-sided conclusions. yet states are fallible and can fail grievously. Just as natural law does not rule out the possibility of just rebellion, so it cannot rule out the possibility of supplying arms which out properly to be borne by the state.

These idealised and perhaps unavoidably pompous remarks about state responsibilities are well worth contrasting with some of the scandals touched upon in other chapters. Clearly, government doses not always judiciously with numerous factors before determining where arms should go. All too often, it scrambles to clinch a deal for narrowly political or commercial reasons. Such conduct is widely regarded as normal and is often thought to become problematic only if "our weapons are used against our boys". when this happens, acquiescence in sleaze gives way to outrage.

The indignation when weapons that we have supplied are used to kill our soldiers I keenly felt but incomprehensible. If the weapons that have killed our sons are of a superior kind then the indignation might be understandable, for we might hypothesize that they would not have defied our enemies had lacked our guns. But this is often not the case. It is the very fact that the weapon was "made in Birmingham" that is felt to be outrageous. Why" If our enemies are using our weapons then we are in the best possible position to understand and thus, to counter the technology that we are up against. And if our economy is the beneficiary of our enemy's military expenditure, how can it be anything but mindless sentimentality to complain? So long as attention is focused exclusively on the nature of the weapons concerned, these questions can be answered only in terms of superstition. For many people, "our" weapons are a potent expression of who "we" are and it is somehow contrary to the magical significance with which we endow the weapons to find them turned against us. May discussions with people of various ages, with and without military experience, have mad em fairly confident that there is in many of us, an object fetishism which makes us object irrationally when our weapons kill our boys. This particular kind of anger does not arise f the weapons have been captured, We somehow fell that is peculiarly repugnant if the weapons have fallen into our enemy's hands by purchase that we have allowed or profited by.

What is so odd about this sentiment is that it is combined with comfortable acquiescent in the most cynical of arms trade strategies. While the weapons are sold, they leave the country as mere merchandise. While they are used by foreigners against one another, we the suppliers, are felt to be uninvolved. If they are turned against us, they acquire enough magical significance to energize many a scandal.

At the end of this chapter, I shall suggest that there is indeed grave reason for concern if weapons that we have sold are used against us, but the reason is quite incompatible with the indifference that attends the weapons' export and use against foreigners. It seems that object fetishism, disconnected from proper moral concerns, powers much of the public outrage when our weapons are used against our boys.

I have suggest that the arms trade is properly regulated by government because it is states that have the power and authority of supply and deny arms as well-informed judgment requires. The high-mindedness of this argument has required a corrective dose of realism which has led us to notice a curious incongruity in the public attitudes which allow cynical practices to be punctuated by scandals when our weapons are turned against us. My suggestion is that these public attitudes are shaped by object fetishism. If this is credit, then we need to look else-

where than to popular sentiment for a realistic appraisal of governments' authority to regulate the arms trade. Where we might we look?
    One possibility is a utilitarian argument that the world is, all
things considered, a better place because of state regulation of the arms
trade. Such a view cannot but seem problematic nowadays, when it is
claimed in an ever wider front that the market place is a better regu-
lator than government intervention. Who knows whether the overall
outcome would be better if the arms trade was entrusted to international markets with minimum regulation? I have seen no study of the
question on other chapters of this book make plain that every sort of
objective study of the arms trade is fraught with difficulty. Personally, I believe that the efficiency of real markets has been greatly
overstated, but this is a personal prejudice which the reader may not
share. It is an open question where government interference in the arms
trade is better than a free market in arms and one which may perhaps
be worth further study. For the purpose of this chapter, I shall assume
that a utilitarian justification of state regulation cannot be assumed.
    Another possible justification of state control of the arms trade is
that non-regulation would allow private persons to exert undue influence on the control of policy. If we allow our arms salesmen t proceed
with little or no regulation, then it is perhaps all too likely that they
will get into scrapes that will involve the state. This we cannot allow,
it might be thought, for no individual or group of individuals can be
permitted to be so dominant in the conduct of foreign affairs. On reflection, such an argument is unconvincing. Individuals and groups of individuals engage in numerous other foreign transactions without achieving undue influence over foreign policy. it is only if the arms trade has
a special significance for some other reason that it can make sense to
think of our arms trader as involving the state in ways that require
state supervision. It is because the arms trade is like no other, because
it is inherently a state affair, that state supervision is required.
    Before we take leave of he private arms supplier to examine the
inescapably public nature of the trade, let us glance briefly a the
closely related matter of unemployment. Firms or worker whose jobs
depend on arms sales may sometimes have very considerable clout, but
do they have any right to this" It is hard to believe that they do. It
may well be that soldiers have a special claim in that they have
pledge their lives to the defence of their country so that there is something peculiarly shabby about their being transferred from he front
line to the ranks of the unemployed. But arms manufacture involves no
special risk to life and limb. Once we set aside any magical significance that my flow from weapons to their makers (as in films of the
factories or yards from which aircraft or shops of past wars came), it
is hard to think of munitions worker as having any special claim to
continued employment.

How, in general, one should regard unemployment is an interesting question beyond the scope of this chapter. Personally, I remain committed to the idea of full employment and am by no means, convinced by the arguments against it of recent years. Nor am I convinced that full employment can be sustained only be acceptance of noxious practices such as the trade in hard drugs, the export of poisonous waste to countries that lack the political culture to resist, or an irresponsible trade in arms. It is certainly not obvious that it can be any more legitimate to remedy or avert unemployment by the arms trade than by these other noxious practices. This applies to whole regions or newly independent states as well as to particular towns or smaller constituencies. Work is an important constituent of what people do with their lives and we do a person a very ill service by allowing illegitimate activities to become or remain the only alternative to unemployment. The task for trade unions and others that have at heart the well-being of individual workers is to find kinds of work that can be performed without shame.

Let us now turn from groups and individuals within society to the state. Why do states export arms beyond the frontiers of formal alliances, such as NATO? To some extent such exports are influence, motivated, driven by interest groups such as the military-industrial complex, but these private interests are never wholly dominant. They are obliged to conceal or represent what they are doing as being in the public interest and it is with the latter that we are here concerned. To the extent that the arms trade can be justified as public policy, the many particular justifications are varied mixtures of influence and economic benefit. Influence tends to depend on the recipient's being able to find alternative suppliers, for no sovereign state is likely to be comfortable with being dependent on one particular supplier.

A special case is the pariah state, isolated from what we politely call the international community and unable to avoid dependence on a particular supplier. The pragmatic politician is bound to be cautious about supplying arms to a pariah to the extent that the international community has the power to make its displeasure felt, but this counsel of prudence cannot be a complete guide to the proper treatment of pariahs. It is perfectly possible for a pariah state to be in the right, a blameless victim of international ostracism, and in such a case pragmatic caution may need in all conscience to be controlled by principle to the extent that it is necessary to supply the pariah.

It is conceivable that this can be done only in secret, involving deception. Various sorts of deception are possible. What they have in common is that they are corrosive of public trust. The public cannot be trusted to support the decent but painful thing that we are doing (e.g. in supplying arms to a pariah state) and so we do it in secret. The need for such action cannot be ruled out a priori.

What can be realistically condemned, however, is the tendency for secrecy and deception to spread far wider than the irreducible minimum. The number of pariah states is bound to be very small in comparison with the total number of states with which a substantial arms suppliers might be motivated to trade. And when secret dealings do come into the open, they do not usually turn out to constitute a noble conspiracy to help some needy party, such as a blameless pariah. As the case discussed in other chapters illustrate, when scandals do occur, public response tends to be remarkably relayed, for the public is comfortable with politicians of whom it s opinion tends towards contempt, and what comes to light is usually a case of grubby opportunism rather than of a high-minded commitment beyond what the public could be expected to bear.

The place of foreign policy deceptions in the development of public cynicism about politics should not be exaggerated lest we fall into the kind of shrill moralizing that tends to conceal the most important realities. In truth, the symbiosis of low popular expectations and sleazy politics has numerous sources among with the conduct of foreign policy is unlikely to be among the most important (witness the truism that are a few votes in foreign policy). The need to raise the standard of both public expectation and the ambition of politicians and civil servants is a general one, as is the need for politicians and civil servants in whom principle is so sound and so much in control that their pragmatism is worth calling prudence. As regards to secrecy and deception tin the arms trade this could in theory be motivated with a high-minded concern to , for example, provide decent support for a pariah state. But in practice, I can think of no modern example of its doing so, and none was suggested at the seminar from which this book flowed. So much for deception.

If there is proper governmental control of the arms trade then there are people - ministers and civil servants - whose job it is to exercise this control. The scope for them to do so is not confined to avoidance of clearly illegal or manifestly dodge (scandal-risking) deals. Governments are in a position to be better informed that their publics about the likely significance of arms sales and transfers. It is for them to exercise this trust with greater or lesser diligence. The Conservative and Labour, has not been encouraging in this regard. The view has been that the arms trade is a legitimate trade of which we seek our fair share. Such a commercial form of words can hardly fit to have a corrupting influence for this is no ordinary trade and those with responsibility for its control need a constant keen awareness of its peculiarities, which are unlikely to be pressed upon them by contemporary elite or mass attitudes. They need to remember the salient principles but what are these principles? This brings me at last to the core of my argument.

In supplying arms, we make ourselves a party to any conflict in which those arms are likely to be uses. This is why the arms trade is different from formal alliances, such as NATO. In the latter, we are already, by treaty, parties to the conflict (I will consider a counter-example at the end of this chapter). In supplying arms, we are doing something of the utmost significance. If an individual supplies arm to another, then the supplier must exercise extreme caution lest he or she become an accessory to murder. When a state supplies arms beyond existing alliances, its right to do so normally derives form its making the legitimate judgment that the recipient deserve support in the conflict(s) for which the arms are likely to be used. The arms trade ought to be an alliance-like activity and one reason for so many shady deals is that such implications are being deliberately evaded. If there is such a thing as a just war, just rebellion, just counter-rebellion, then it seems very likely that there is such things as a just arms sale, but just wars, etc., are rare. Justifiable alliances are rare, and by the same token it is no light matter to accede to the sale or transfer of arms. To think of the arms trade as a legitimate trade of which we seek our fair share is corrupting, because it represents something which should be rare and weighty as being a legitimately everyday occurrence, like selling sweets. The realization that tin supplying arms we make ourselves a party t any conflict in which the arms are likely to be used is thus a challenging possible starting point for public and official thinking on the subject, a genuine alternative to the precarious idea of a legitimate trade in arms.

All doubtful technologies are included in the formula to the extent that they too involve something all too like the hazard of supplying arms to a likely murderer. This does not mean, however, a cessation of all economic relationships. There is a great difference between exercising caution lest one become an accessory to murder and indulging in the fantasy that one has an obligation to identify all possible murders beforehand and to subject them to effective dissuasion, or at least to cut off all normal relationships. A person whom we must needs treat with caution, lest we become an accessory to murder may well not yet have committed any such crime, and what is material to the dead is, n any case, only a tiny subset of the totality of economic requirements of the suspicious person. He or she requires food and drink, shelter, etc., and it is only to the extent that a particular item is in the given context suspect that it can be sensible for us to be wary of becoming accessories to murder.

Thus the list of suspect items may well be narrower than COCOM's Cold War list, which seems to have been more like a recipe for (not necessarily illegitimate) active economic warfare than a cautious avoidance of involvement in other people s injustices. To confine one's sale and transfer of arms and related technology, training, etc. to that which could be justified as formal alliance is one thing; to undertake warfare against a particular state is another; and between the two is an area of great importance in which the state carefully refrains from making itself a party to potentially or actually murderous conflict through the arms trade without thereby joining the struggle by economic warfare. A relatively uncontroversial general principle is that as one state has the sovereign right o refuse them. On way in which this general sovereign right might be exercised is by prudent caution to avoid both becoming an accessory to murder an being taken in by unwarranted accusations of economic warfare. Free trade does not mean free trade in arms.

Although the sovereign right to refuse to sell arms I uncontroversial, many of us are distinctly uncomfortable with the paternalism (which would better be called parentalism for this is no feminist issue) of our being the judges of their states' security needs. In truth, the challenge to avoid becoming an accessory to murder is not a call to paternalism, but it is well worth noticing that there is one kind of case in which the will to bring the arms trade under prudent control can explicitly involve respect for the political inner workings of the arms purchaser There are cases in which the purchasing country possesses an opposition party which is playing an effective part in the political process by which the purchase is authorized. In such a case, we might make it a principle that arms, raining, etc. are to be provided only if they are know and approved by the opposition as well as by the government. This would be a necessary and not a sufficient condition, for there is nothing magic about any political process and the most perfect of political constitutions is capable of playing host to murder. But where there are opposition politicians who are engaged in the debates that authorise government action, it might well be sensible to regard their access to information and their attitudes as a good indicator of what is suspect by way of arms trading.

There are so many cases in which effective opposition within the purchasing state is lacking, that one is tempted to seek general guidelines. One thought worth considering s that in such cases, the supplier should normally insist on a true cash deal as a safeguard against the many instances of sales and transfers that involve secret politics, covert interests and blatant corruption within the supplier and or recipient. Alas, such a proposal sounds utopian. It is not that the sales and transfers need to be secret for military reasons: in general, it is open, public transfers that enhance deterrence by showing the potential aggressor that the costs of attack are too high. It is the politics of the arms trade that militates against openness, not least when the secretive purchaser is buying domestic legitimization by demonstrating to its own elites the continued support of foreign interest-groups. It seems to me that no general guidelines are feasible in the absence of effective opposition within the recipient state. All that we can do is to exercise prudence on two fronts, striving to ensure both that we do not become accessories to murder and that we do not fail to supply arms on the rare occasions when they, like formal alliances I other cases, are what is required within the well-known principles of just war and just rebellion.

My argument has been a general one, applicable to all states alike, as natural law arguments of principle are bound to be. What, it might be asked, has this to do with the European arms trade? I have given reason for doubting that anything can be learnt form a hypothetical European idea and I have conceded nothing to distinctively European current conditions, such as concerns the unemployment of Cold War minions workers. What remains to consider is that we Europeans are not the only arms suppliers, so that if we exercise prudence, it by no means follows that others will do likewise: "If we don't do it, someone else will". If my argument carries conviction, then we can place this question within a context that starkly clarifies the issues. The question is not a merely emotive one, such as "How would you feel if weapons supplied by you were used against your own side?". for we are not discussing the magic significance that is projected into or weapons by object fetishism. The question is not a blandly easy one, for the arms trade cannot be a legitimate trade of which we seek our fair share. The question is whether we are prepared to become accessories t murder on the excuse that others are prepared to do so. Put like this, the question should answer itself, for murder is still murder, whoever acquiesces in it. If we Europeans are unwilling to do so, it is not because we are better tan anyone else, but because anyone can tell you that murder is a very serious matter, whether the law against it is enforced or not.

Let me conclude with a further brief remark about realism, for it is realists who are likely to be the most effective critics of the sort of argument that I have attempted to sketch. Twentieth-century English-language realists have often doubted the ability of public opinion to cope with the challenges of foreign policy. They have found ample reason to contrast foolish popular moralizing with an awareness of realities and dilemmas which is confined to elites. They have been less successful in recognizing that elites are many, and are often foolish and blinkered, but their insistence that it is mere sentimentality to look for wisdom in public agreements publicly arrived at poses a serious challenge to the kind of preference for principled public positions that I have sought to apply to the arms trade. What needs emphasis above all, is that a natural law argument such as the one I have outlined, attributes magical powers of wisdom to no particular par to the body politic. Prudence in the arms trade is made more difficult and less likely if ministers and civil servants deceive themselves about basic moral realities by spicing webs of half truth and evasion. It is also

made more difficult and less likely if public opinion is cynical and in-
different. We are more likely, and never certain, to hit the mark if all
parts of the body politic take serious the same simple principles.
Pragmatic realists need not disagree with this unless their minds are I
thrall to an excessively static or cynical conception of human nature.

I have tried to bring out the central moral issue in the European
arms trade by relating it to the seriousness of formal alliances. Here
again, realist may raise a quizzical eyebrow. Even if they grant that
NATO is an altogether more serious kind of commitment than the
eighteenth century alliances which were begun and ended with promis-
cuous ease, they my well point out that NATO's principal members
have no wish for the alliance to embroil them in the vicious conflict
between Greece and Turkey. I agree about the wish and very much
hope that we may continue to be spared the kinds of hard choices that
are all too easy to imagine. but it seems fair to add that the very logic
of NATO is such that intensification of Greece-Turkish conflict would
not but challenge the viability of NATO by forcing us to clarify our
commitments, commitments which are already real and substantial. My
point is that the arms trade is as serious a commitment as this, though
obfuscating rhetoric serves to conceal the fact.

SUBJECT INDEX

arms embargo, 12
arms transfers, 135
competitiveness of the
international arms trade, 101
economic benefit.i.s, 17
Gulf War, 7
Accountability, 13, 24
Advanced Electronics Center, 82
advanced technology, 17
Aerospatiale, 6
Aérospatiale, 55
Aérospatiale`s, 45
Africa, 49, 101
agricultural commodities, 75
Airbus civil aircraft production,
43
Alenia, 43
Apache missile, 51
Arab states, 127
"areas of tension" criteria, 33
Argentina, 36
Armament Agency, 54
Arms and Yugoslavia, 132
arms categories, 92
arms control, 22
arms export, 56
Arms Export Control Act, 76
Arms Export Policy, 103
Arms exports, 17, 18, 48
arms restraint, 26
arms sales policy audit, 24

arms trade controls, 16
arms transfer controls, 23
arms transfers, 22, 25, 35, 74, 98,
101, 131, 141
Arrangement on Guidelines for
Officially Supported Export
Credits, 75
Asian Pacific, 20
Association of South-East Asian
Nations, 36
ASTRID, 50
Australia Group's, 61
Austria, 138

Bank of Credit and Commerce
International, 74
barter, 75
Bavaria, 36
Belgian, 9
Bosnia, 135, 136, 140
Bosnian Muslims, 147
Brazil, 36
British Aerospace, 6, 23, 83
British arms trade, 28
British interest in the Gulf, 121
British Petroleum, 83

capability, 116
cartelization, 6

categories of equipment, 101
CFE Treaty, 38
chemical warfare, 116
chemical weapons, 61
China, 63, 69
CIEEMG, 48, 49
Clinton Nonproliferation, 65
CMEA, 80
co-production deals, 22
Co-production,, 75
COCOM, 63
COCOM country list, 35
COCOM's, 152
Code of Conduct on Arms
Exports, 25
COFACE, 78
Cold War, 88, 90
Cold War list, 152
Common Foreign and Security
Policy (CFSP), 141
Conservative-Liberal coalition,
36
contracts, 114
conventional Forces in Europe, 4
conventional weapon systems
proliferation, 22
conventional weapons
proliferation, 13
coordinate licensing, 8
coproduction agreements, 25
coproduction of the equipment,
81
Council for Mutual Economic
Assistance, 79
counterproliferation, 67
countertrade, 75, 81
Credit Financing, 19
Croatia, 133, 137
cross border integration, 4
CSBMs, 102
CSCE, 102
customs control, 8
Czech Republic, 139

Daimler Benz, 44
DASA, 6, 43, 45
Dassault Aviation, 51
DCN, 51
DCNI, 51
deception, 151
Defence Export Sales
Organisation, 2, 18
Defence Export Services
Organisation, 19
Defence Exports Services
Organisation (DESO), 110
Defence Exports Services
Secretariat (DESS), 110
Defense Production Act, 82
Defense Security Assistance
Agency, 76
Delegation Generale pour
l'Armement, 2
Department of Trade and
Industry (DTI), 110
DESO, 15, 19, 111, 115, 126
DESS, 111
Deutsche Aerospace, 55
DGA, 49
Domestic Public Opinion, 117
DTI, 110, 126
dual use export policy, 65
dual-use goods, 35
dual-use goods and
technologies, 8
dual-use technology, 38, 68
dual-use technology transfers, 8
"dual-use" trade., 16

E-3 Sentry AWACS, 82
Export Controls, 24
EC, 47
EC governments, 101
Economic Motives, 123
Economic Support Fund, 76
EFTA states, 95
ELAs, 127
end-user certificates, 139

enforcement policies, 8
Enhanced Proliferation Control
Initiative, 60
Ethics, 143
Eureka, 7
Eurocopter, 45, 55
Euromissile, 55
European Armament Agency., 54
European Arms Trade, 1
European Commission, 7, 55, 60
European Community, 62
European defence industry, 5
European dual-use technology, 8
European Fighter Aircraft, 3
European regulation, 41
European Suppliers, 4
European Union, 42, 141
Europeanization, 53
Excess Defense Articles (EDA)
programme, 76
Eximbank, 18
export credit, 74
Export Credit Guarantee
Department, 15, 18, 19
Export Credit Guarantee
Department in the UK, 78
export defence equipment, 115
export financing, 80, 84
Export Financing in the
Transition Economies, 79
export of Goods (Control) Order
1980, 106
export guidelines, 16
export licensing, 14
export of weapon production
facilities, 38
export orders, 15
Export Regulations, 32, 41, 45
Export restrictions, 26
Export-Import Bank, 77

Far East, 96, 101
FCO, 110
Federal Financing Bank, 77

Financing the Arms Trade, 71
Foreign and Commonwealth
Office (FCO), 110
Foreign Military Finance
programme., 76
Foreign Military Financing
programme, 76
Foreign Military Sales (FMS)
programme, 76
foreign policy deceptions, 151
Foreign Trade Act, 32, 38, 42
former East German Army, 40
France high-tech industries, 50
Franco-German Armament
Agency, 54
French Arms Trade, 47
French defence industries, 51
French MoD, 49
French SOFMA, 78

G-7, 60
GATT, 84
GEC, 23, 83
General Agreement on Tariffs
and Trade, 3
General Dynamics, 82
General Peoples Defence, 132
German Arms Export Policy, 31,
39
German Industry Association, 44
German Ministry of Finance, 78
German rearmament, 32
Germany's arms industry, 31
GIAT, 6
GICAT, 50
GIE, 55
government-to-government co-
production projects, 45
Greece, 98
Guidelines, 116
Guidelines on Nuclear
Transfers., 59
Gulf, 122
Gulf region, 36

Gulf War, 9, 67, 88
Hallstein Doctrine, 35
Hawk aircraft, 118
Heckler and Koch, 12
Hercegovina, 135
Hercules transport, 55
Hermes, 78
Hermes credit guarantee
programe, 78
Hidden Cost of the Arms
Trade, 17
high technology, 18
human rights, 16
Hungary, 80

illegal transfers, 35
Illicit Arms, 127
Indian central bank., 80
Indian nuclear test in 1974, 58
Indirect offsets, 20
Indonesia, 16
Influence, 120
insurance for transfers, 78
international arms sales, 28
International Atomic Energy
Agency, 59
International Military
Education and Training, 76
International Opinion, 119
international transparency, 26
Iran, 23, 36, 104, 108, 112, 115,
120, 127, 139
Iran-Iraq, 123
Iraq, 16, 23, 62, 64, 67, 74, 78,
104, 108, 114, 115, 120
Iraq invasion of Kuwait, 33
Iraqi arms market, 23
Italian Banca Nazionale del
Lavoro, 74

Jordan, 36

Kalashnikov automatic rifles,
133, 139
KONVER, 7
Kurds, 119

Latin America, 78
League of Nations, 89
Leclerc tanks, 49
Libya, 34
licenses for exports, 8
Loans, 19
London Club, 59

M-1 Abrams tank, 82
M1 Abrams tank, 95
Maastricht conference, 54
Maastricht Treaty, 62, 64
Maastrict Treaty, 6
machine tools, 114
Malaysia, 16
Malaysian deal, 23
manufacturing employment, 17
Martin Marieta, 56
Matra, 6
MATRA Défense Espace, 51
Matra Marconi Space, 55
Matrix Churchill affair., 13
Matrix Churchill machine
tools, 111, 114
Mediterranean Basin, 49
Middle East, 2, 20, 28, 88, 96,
101, 126
Middle-East, 49
MiG-29 fighter aircraft, 80, 81
Military Assistance Programe,
77
Military Assistance
Programme, 76
military transfer agreements, 2
Ministry of Defence (MOD), 110
MOD, 110
MOD Arms Working Party
(AWP), 110

MOD Working Group, 110
MODWG, 115
morality of arms trading, 144
multilateral arms embargoes, 22

National Audit Office, 19
NATO, 6, 32, 36, 60, 84, 96, 143
NATO countries, 38
NATO,, 76
natural law arguments, 154
Netherlands, 9
Nigeria, 36
Nonproliferation, 58
nonproliferation export controls, 69
North Africa, 28
North American Free Trade Agreement, 69
North Korea, 62, 67
nuclear exports, 59
nuclear security, 67
Nuclear Suppliers Group, 59, 61

OECD, 75
Office for Technology Assessment, 81
Office of Disarmament Affairs, 99
Offsets, 20, 74, 81, 83, 85
oil, 122
OPEC countries, 36
Operation Staunch, 107

P5 process, 94
Pacific Asia, 2
Panavia of British Aerospace, 43
Panel of Experts, 93
parliament, 26
parliamentary accountability, 14

participation, 101
Pergau Dam affair, 7, 14
Pergau dam scandal, 22
PERIFRA, 7
Petersburg declaration, 54
Pinochet regime, 16
Plessey, 5
Post Cold War Era, 57, 60
Post-Cold War Era, 4
production.i., 38
proliferation, 60
proliferation of conventional weapons, 22
Public opinion, 118

realism, 144
Regional Marketing Desks for Iran and Iraq, 110
Regional Stability, 121
regulating global trade, 85
Release of Military Information Policy Committee (RMIPC), 110
research and development costs, 18
Russia, 79, 80, 94
Russian banks, 80

Safeguards, 59, 63
safeguards on nuclear transfers., 59
sales bans, 35
Saudi Arabia, 12, 36, 82, 83, 109, 124
scandals, 147
Scott Inquiry, 13
secrecy, 28, 151
secret arms transfers, 138
Selenia, 6
Siemens, 5
Singapore, 141
Single European Act, 7
Single European Market, 5

Slovakia, 80
Slovenia, 133
SOGEPA, 51
South Africa, 16
southeast Asia, 75
state regulation of the arms
trade, 149
supply of spares, 114

Taiwan, 88
tank producers, 41
Third World, 28, 36
Thompson-CSF, 6
Thomson, 56
Tornado fighter aircraft, 43
Tornado fighter planes, 36
transatlantic arms transfers, 3
transfers of defense equipment,
84
Transparency, 13, 24, 99, 102
Transparency in Armaments, 91
Treaty of Rome, 7
Treaty on Conventional Armed
Forces in Europe, 40

U.K. and, 103
U.K.'s Arms Trade Policy, 11
U.N. Register, 87
UK Arms Market, 28
UK arms trade, 13
UK Defence Export Services
Organisation, 78
UK export policies, 23
UK's arms export policy, 105
UK's arms trade policy, 24
Uk's Defence Export Policy
Towards Iran And Iraq, 117
Ukrainian defence industry, 79
UN Arms Trade Register, 26
UN embargo, 137
UN First Committee, 91
UN Group of Experts, 89

UN Office of Disarmament
Affairs, 93
UN Register on Conventional
Weapons, 24
United Nations Register of
Conventional Arms., 38
United Nations Register of
Conventional Weapons, 31
United Nations Security
Council, 60
United Nations Security
Council Resolution 687, 61
United States, 38, 57, 66
Unites States Export Financing,
76
UNPROFOR, 137, 141
US AMRAAM, 51
US F-15 aircraft, 88
US Office of Management and
Budget, 82

Visegrad four,, 95

Warsaw Pact organization, 143
Warsaw Treaty Organisation,
90
Warsaw Treaty Organization,
79
WEAG, 54
Weapon Systems, 18, 95
weapon types, 101
Weapons of War Control Act,
32
West European Armament
Group, 54
West European Countries, 78
Western European Union, 6
WEU, 56

Yugoslav People's Army, 132
Yugoslavia, 131